SHAPES *of* TRUTH

SHAPES
of TRUTH

Discover God Inside You

Neal Allen

Pearl Publications

Pearl Publications
Fairfax, California

©2021 by Neal Allen
neal@shapesoftruth.com
www.shapesoftruth.com

Library of Congress Control Number: 2021900522

ISBN: 978-0-578-83908-0

For Renata, Andrew, Marina and David

Contents

❧

Foreword

Pearl

A Buddhist, a Christian, a Jew, a misanthrope and a secular humanist walk into a bar. This isn't a joke, but a description of the audience for the book in your hands. Anyone interested in life, love, truth, transformation and simply being humans together will find it exhilarating, will be changed and challenged and nourished by its insights. The book bridges two camps often considered at odds with each other – rationalists and the spiritually inclined – with its elucidation of a recent discovery that can widen our understanding of truth. You can explore what's in the book on your own, in the momentousness of dealing with everyday life, or in more reflective times to assist in finding meaning, or peace or God in the world. In *Shapes of Truth*, the accountant and his Burning Man, yoga-obsessed daughter will find something they both can talk about.

Full disclosure. The author is my husband.

The first thing I noticed when I laid eyes on Neal Allen in 2016 was what a good nose he has, and large, beautiful hands. Within a few minutes, I could see that he had a high intelligence, possible over-education, and a broad range of interests; before our coffee cups were half empty we had covered Kierkegaard, *Les Enfants du Paradis* and JonBenét Ramsey. He was gentle and kind, a little shambly, very observant, and an excellent listener. He was droll but subtle about it.

I was a tiny bit discombobulated, and not just because it was, after all, a first date. My problem was less romantic; that very morning I had decided to fire a longtime assistant. As I settled into my seat at the restaurant, I felt down and guilty. Being me, I might have mentioned this in passing with Neal. He didn't recoil at the over-share, or express knee-jerk sympathy at my distress, so much as he seemed deeply curious. So curious that I had a hard time changing the subject.

After our second cup of coffee, we got to down to the books we were each writing. His was called *Shapes of Truth*.

Oh, I asked prettily, "What is it about?"

"Let me show you," he offered, and began to walk me through the process that he describes in the book. He told me to think about my difficulty that morning with my assistant. I closed my eyes to begin the interior visualization. He asked if I felt anything distinctive in my torso, and if so, where was it? I described a cramped feeling in my lower belly, anxiety I had over the firing. Neal asked me to describe the exact size of the area of tension, the shape of the area, its density, and its color. It was an ugly stain, a spilled liquid, grayish brown, the density of mercury. He asked me to stay with it for a minute. I desperately wanted to run, but I sat quietly, partly because of the cute nose, but also because my stomach felt terrible and maybe this would help. Then I noticed the strangest thing, that the gray-brown liquid was floating in an empty space, as if some of my internal organs had been pushed aside and had left behind a pristine staging area.

After a while he asked if the thing in my belly was changing in any way. Well, not fast enough, I can tell you that. But in fact, it had changed slightly, and continued to, becoming wider and less dense, less like mercury. Then after some time, it rose higher, eventually reaching my chest, much airier now, and then slowly rose up my throat, and into the air beside me, where it disappeared.

In its place I noticed a white balloon.

An icky, thick, grayish-brown blob had transformed through attention into a white balloon, hovering beside me and then magically inside me, too.

"Ah," Neal said, smiling. "You went straight to the Pearl."

"The Pearl?"

"Yeah," he said. "The Pearl – that white balloon – is kind of like looking straight at your own soul, or at least a part of it, as if you can see both your own divinity and your ability to function in the world from your divinity."

Neal's little parlor trick took me from my familiar self as an anxious, cranky adult full of self-doubt and blame to my own patch of the sacred. In about ten minutes. So yeah, I wanted to go out with him again, which we did the next day, and every day since.

Neal told me the Sufi story of the pearl without price. Soon after the prince's birth, his mother and father, the king and queen, move to a new dominion far away. When the prince comes of age, the king and queen command him to leave the castle and retrieve a treasure box from the town where he was born. With scant instructions and an unreliable map, the boy makes his way back, encountering dangers and obstacles all along the way. When he finds the treasure box and opens it, a perfect white pearl is revealed, which he carries with him as he returns home to the castle, and holds forever after. It's the story of the journey to recover our birthright to our own perfection and holiness.

My experience on our first date, it turns out, was pretty standard in a mind-blowing way – standard in the sense that as you will find in *Shapes of Truth*, this is a simple, mechanical, and previously unknown way to bring the divine into your life at your own pace and as you need it. Besides being a breezy introduction to my husband's curious universe, the book is a practical, step-by-step guide and exploration of a mostly unknown method of dialogue and meditation, which sneakily leads to breakthrough.

So what was it like for me, Al Franken, a follower of Jesus, to encounter this material the first time? One might think I would have wanted to run screaming for my cute little Christian life, to my identity as a child of God, part of the Body of Christ. But instead, I felt exhilarated, freed from bondage to my emotional rejection of both my self and my employee. I got incredibly happy.

Now we are married and spend our lives together, and I'll tell you all about that another time. But this is about Neal's book. Of course I was predisposed to love *Shapes of Truth*. But by the same token, I was extremely anxious about reading it, in case it was too woo-woo, overwrought, esoteric, pedantic, intellectual, or poorly written. To my great relief and pleasure, it is the opposite of all these things, a brilliantly written and welcoming work. Neal's writing is fresh and exhilaratingly erudite, capable at times of namedropping Plato and Chomsky but with the conversational charms of Bill Bryson. Plus, he has stolen several of my best lines, although I am too nice and too in love to call him on this.

Get ready for a roller coaster ride as Neal describes the timeless body-forms, their everyday appearance in his coaching practice, and his own personal search for truth and healing. What makes the book thrilling is the bandwidth of his spiritual understanding, his great sense of humor, and his ability to explain the esoteric while singing the plainsong of universal truth.

And the core subject matter is pretty good, too: Neal learned much of it from Hameed Ali, whose Diamond Approach path led Neal deeply into spiritual realms for ten years.

Diamond Approach is very different from my primary path, Christianity, but not hard for me to assimilate. Neal and I converge on secondary paths – Ram Dass, meditation, sitting with dying people, Scandinavian crime TV, and the surprising discovery late in life that the ultimate and only reality is Love. In recognizing our commonalities I'm not talking about tolerance for each other's faith, like inviting my Jewish friends to Christmas brunch or nodding along as my chart is being read, or any of the ways I can remain cheerily smug in knowing the truth while pretending to acknowledge another's. Nor am I talking about Neal's and my occasional brief conversations about Merton or St. John the Divine or Ramana Maharshi.

It's deeper. We both believe that Love is not an emotion, but the ground of our being, and that which unites all of us, removing all separation. We have studied and internalized many of the same wisdom teachings, just taught differently to each of us. We are on the same sheet of music: love, truth, heart, innocence, soul, union.

It turns out that by holding our own primary paths lightly – I'm not such a big fan of the church as I am of my buddy Jesus – we have room to go deep into other ways of truth.

Neal and I recently vacationed in Israel. For me, the high point was bathing in the Jordan River, where Jesus was baptized and cleansed as he prepared to go out and teach. I waded into the river in my street clothes and with little thought found myself immersed head to toe. Neal objected to the fish nibbling at his ankles and got out before the water reached knee high. He loves Jesus, but not the way I do. Plus he is a big baby.

That same day in Israel, we visited a site in Haifa, the Shrine of the Bab. It's the final resting place for the forerunner to the founder of the Baha'i faith, a one-room white marble mausoleum surrounded by infinitely terraced and impeccably maintained gardens.

Neither of us is Baha'i, nor versed in its beliefs and practices. But we both experienced a deeply moving sweetness and stillness in the tomb. God was not just present, but flashing us. And by our both being there for the show, we amplified its sanctity in each other, and murmured about it with wide teary eyes afterward. That's how two people on different paths can meet in the deeper realms.

Which is to say that Neal's unique practice and his book can resonate with most anyone on any spiritual path. Before Neal came into my life I had never encountered a process like his, where these deeply and so-often-disappointing bodies of ours hold some of the greatest tools to understanding the nature of truth, of soul, of Self.

His mentor Ali's discovery, as expressed through Neal's writing, is easy to grok, in its simplicity and depth. And it is so moving as the expression of the hidden deeper reality we carry within us.

Close up Neal writes about tough human predicaments – loss, break-up, jealousy, limbo – but instead of bogging down in difficulty as pain, this work seems to release a kind of joy in encountering truth. I'm freed from spending a lot of time on the How and Why, and instead encounter an unexpected *What Is*. It's not that I don't learn things when Neal does one of these body-based visualizations with me, especially things about my past, but I get to go through them to a more primordial me, outside time and space, who is a lot more interesting than the person who wanted to see my employee atone for her sins. The white balloon of me is just as real and present and active as the guilt-ridden, sulking, familiar self.

You and I don't have to give anything up about who we are, what we do, and how we move through the world. All this work does is add to that. For instance, I can now resist despots, and at the same time feel deep compassion for their isolation.

Or this: Buying Pepto Bismol can lead to a loving exchange with the 7-Eleven clerk, because we've moved into the theater of soul, even while I'm living in the world of people and drama, and fishing around in my purse for exact change. Love and respect can show up in the most commonplace moments of time, transformed into wonder, like during my encounter with an unwrapped cough drop from the nineties in the change at the bottom of my purse.

I get to learn about my own qualities, abstracted and discriminated into pure essences. When I learn about true strength, I don't have to fake it, and try to get my way or win. I can still be sweet, even while appropriately holding my own. I don't have to force my will when I recognize and connect with the natural steadfastness that is actually already within me. These essential forms, LEGO blocks of strength and sincerity, become my foundation.

Something truer overwhelms the belief that I am a limited, deficient human being trying to get things done my way. I experience a lightening, and life becomes more buoyant, more playful. I can feel and see yellow bubbles rising through my body that represent my natural boundless curiosity, that of a child. I notice an unusual access to that which I don't usually see, and encounter awe in finding what is right around me and has been since birth, which has been with me every moment beyond boundaries and limits and demands.

You can tell in these pages that Neal feels blessed to have come upon this transformative work, and that he loves to pass it on. His is not a soupy gratitude for this knowledge. He just thinks it's wonderful to watch people encounter these truths. I observe him do this work with our family and friends when they are stuck or distressed, how dubious they are when he first asks them to close their eyes, and how quiet and amazed they become as things progress. They kind of pink up eventually, like babies.

I watch Neal help people discover that deep down they are already whole, curious, content, and full of vigor. Every time a friend does one of these body form exercises, I see the true self arise, and how she or he gets to feel it and love it and, magically, be it.

This is not a messianic or doctrinal book of teachings. It's the opposite, like a nature walk through a field of your true nature, all the flowers, bushes, thistles, ponds and birds within. Neal has shown me over the past four years that he knows how to roll with whatever comes at him, including the complexities of extended family, and aging, and having a *gifted, beautiful wife*, and I can see that this is a direct result of the work he describes in the book. I really like this guy, and I think you will, too. You hold a certain kind of mojo in your hands.

Anne Lamott
Fairfax, California

Chapter 1

Your Spectacular Interior

This is another book about God.

It's OK if you're nervous about that. I think God should make everyone nervous. We've all been seven-year-olds praying for a bike or happier parents or access to Narnia. And sooner or later, we've all felt betrayed by the God who didn't show up and grant us the wish. In that childhood betrayal, a seed of discontent is planted, which dogs most of us until death. It's been a struggle for everyone from the ancients – think St. Augustine – to your favorite self-help guru. When we're sunk in the morass of personal betrayal, books about God can be an irritation before any kind of a blessing is bestowed. This one has some of that suffering, but the God it opens is light and frothy and even funny.

I use several terms for the reality that God encompasses: God, the divine, and Consciousness are my favorites when writing. Each title evokes a distinct mental picture, but they're all talking about the same thing. For me, "God" still has a big fluffy beard and sits up there in the clouds. "The divine" is sparkly and evanescent and tickles my shoulders. "Consciousness with a capital C" is more like a field that stretches from my neck to the sky and keeps going, knowingly. All or any of the above are fine pictures to have in your mind while following what's being talked about here. I don't care what your religion is, and I don't care if you're an atheist. None of that has any bearing on what I'll cover in this book.

Besides being about God, this is a book about experiences that, as Timothy Leary famously said about LSD, can be better than sex. At least bad sex. And you don't need a bedroom or an especially willing companion to experience them. Anyone can, and it takes no training.

With that much introduction, let's get on with it.

Hidden in your body is a set of thirty-five embodied concepts that describe qualities of God. You can experience them. It's as if you discover God inside you.

These body-forms appear inside your body. When they appear, you have the feeling that part of you was hollowed out, and the body-form is floating inside in 3-D HD. They feel palpable, not imaginary. And they're not just special effects. Experiencing them provides a sense of well-being, respite from day-to-day concerns, and over time can help you land in a life that feels lighter, more loving, and less difficult. They might constitute most of an entire path to enlightenment for you. You just need to know where and how to look for them.

Each body-form represents a simple and easy-to-understand characteristic of the divine. To those of us who experience them, they seem to be universal, specific, and valuable. One might be a red, vibrant sphere sitting in the center of your chest, as if a phantom organ. It shows up for you exactly the same way it shows up for me. It has a meaning – in this case "strength." We share that meaning; when either of us finds the red object, it comes with the feeling that I suddenly know my own capacity for strength. Another might be a dense, ebony mountain rising in your lower abdomen. It likewise has a meaning – "existence." Meeting this mountain inside, we experience a secure understanding of our own inner existence.

These thirty-five embodied concepts, each with its own color and other sensory attributes, don't just describe reality in a peculiarly accurate way; finding them inside you can also grant immediate and, eventually, sustained relief from everyday suffering.

For you, they might feel like a return to a lost land of perfection. Or perhaps as a simple set of building blocks for language. Or an encounter with a trippy, different reality. But they're not just a weird experience; they also seem to have some kind of instructive power. They are all representative of the right side of right versus wrong and the good side of good versus bad. They act as if we operate from an inner goodness. But they're specific enough that they might also relate to the typical binary system that we call morals: good/bad, valuable/worthless, strong/weak, etcetera, the mental workings that allow judgment and decision-making.

If you are like me, you've felt a yearning for what's true and real. You might have been frustrated by the shadows that get in the way. You've sought perfect happiness, perhaps, or some kind of sustained satisfaction, and a pesky difficulty or suffering always seemed to interrupt the possibility. The carnival ride was fun right up to the point when your lunch reared up from your stomach. Still, you've persisted and, in one way or another, at times you've steadied your practical mind. By and large you've gotten your work done, your family raised in an uneasy harmony, your basic needs fulfilled. You know how to do the requirements of life, and maybe a little more. You've paddled a kayak, or driven a go-kart on a slick track, or baked a pie. But some parts of you still feel tentative. Maybe the big questions elude you: Who am I? What's God? What will it be like to die? What will make my children happy? What is greed? What is suffering? What will make *me* happy?

These questions seem to lurk in the shadows, popping up during the most dismal of times. I don't question my happiness while watching a toddler staring into her first noggin-sized mass of pink cotton candy. I don't ask the meaning of life as I'm hanging the decorations for the high school graduation party celebrating the last of my six children. But when I've learned that the neighbor kid has leukemia, I might search for happiness. When I've lost my job, I might search for purpose. We're dark night of the soul people; we rely on times of great suffering to take us to wisdom. That works, but it's patently inefficient. And sleepless nights are no box of kittens.

The body-forms – these thirty-five qualities found inside – light up the world beyond the shadows, and they do it in real time, and they don't require great suffering in order to emerge. They're around, available, all the time, every day, like the rising and setting of the sun. Surprisingly, they are based on words that we all know by heart and whose meanings are so simple that it would be strange to doubt them. This is weird indeed, that I can use some very common words, isolated from much context, and by clearing the way for them to appear in a pure, uncorrupted form, I can find God. Inside little old me.

Think of them as characteristics that might accompany a beneficent God. Or as things that just about everyone naturally values. Or think of them as things that tend to stay, as I said, on the good side of good versus bad judgments, or that stay on the side of right in the fight between right and wrong. You might see them as a one-sided moral compass.

I'm going to first walk you through some of them so that you get an idea of how powerful they might be. After that, we'll get to the surprisingly simple way to evoke them in yourself.

Like any components of language, the vocabulary of the body-forms are *not* the essential aspects of the divine themselves. They are conceptual. A big red ball in my abdomen is no more *strength* in action than the word "strength" is. Like a common word, any individual body-form is only a signifier for something that precedes language or sensation. Strength was here before we had a word or symbol for it. But body-forms are more reliable, and less contaminated, than words. The body-form acts as a bridge between the conceptual world of words that we live in every day and a deeper formless reality that pervades everything.

You can have a vague notion of God but a precise experience of one of the thirty-five body-forms. Each one represents a facet of God that is essential to the human experience. God might be sensed by you today as "power," for instance, and tomorrow as "satisfaction." Power and satisfaction are two of the thirty-five. Each is a way of seeing the divine in everyday life. Each enlivens Consciousness in a particular way. In this cosmology, these words of value are a complete set, a full representation of thirty-five distinct aspects of God that can be found embodied in any human.

Here they are, in their English language form: Joy, Strength, Will, Compassion, Power, Truth, Brilliancy, Value, Knowingness, Personal Love, Passionate Love, Universal Love, Merging Love, Identity, Personal Essence, Universal Will, Existence, Sincerity, Surrender, Melting, Vulnerability, Acceptance, Spirituality, Contentment, Impersonality, Nourishment, Space, Gratitude, Satisfaction, Transparency, Fulfillment, Forgiveness, Death Space, Impeccability, Anointment.

The spectacular discovery of these fundamental principles for life isn't mine. Credit goes to a Berkeley trained physicist who early on turned his attention to psychology and spirituality. His name is Hameed Ali; he writes under the pen name A.H.Almaas. As is true of many scientific breakthroughs, Ali wasn't looking for the essential body-forms, but stumbled upon them while inquiring into other categories of reality.

Ali recognized five of them as interior objects studied by the Sufi since at least the 12th century of the modern era. For the Sufi, who call them the *lataif,* they are subtle organs that are revealed only after much spiritual work. Together, they comprise a subtle body that is hidden within the familiar contour and organs of a human.

But their discovery may go back even farther. Ali and I agree that Plato may have known about them in the 4th century BCE but had his reasons not to write about them.

The body-forms are inborn, and apparently are given to us as the starting point for the business of living our lives. One would think that they should be known to everyone. They form an additional language that we are born with, a quasi-moral vocabulary of value that we don't have to learn from a parent or a pastor or a teacher or a friend or a book. The rules of life are built in.

These thirty-five concepts provide any human with a built-in template for all decision-making, and help to distinguish right from wrong for us, good from bad, and where we want to go next. As far as I can tell, to live is to be in a constant stream of choices. In conjunction with ordinary knowledge, these body-forms can provide an accurate way to make choices.

Learning about these body-forms is superficially similar to a written vocabulary lesson, but the body-forms don't sink in until they are experienced with your senses, in your body. What is that like?

Back when you were an infant, you spent some time inside and then out of the womb without learning words. You were immersed in a world that was a pervasive, seamless film of sights and sounds, smells and tastes, with shapes and tones and wafting odors moving and changing, never quite landing and never harming you. You did not have distinct objects, or a sense of one thing being separated from another. It all flowed together.

Before you got to know the world in a socially relevant way, you encountered it directly through your senses. An overhead light would shine brightly, and not knowing what a *lamp* is or what *shining* is or that there are *colors*, you would simply aim your eyes at the light and stare at it for as long as it occupied your attention.

You were an explorer without a goal, a being of pure curiosity.

You stayed in contact with the experiences that evoked pleasure, and moved away from contact with painful experiences. Mostly you just flowed with what was coming and going, experiencing the qualities that appeared briefly to your senses.

You also exhibited instinctual patterns that helped you get fed, changed, to sleep, warmed, cooled, loved and cared for.

The thirty-five abstract body-forms are like that. Imagine if the word "strength" dropped from your mind, but instead appeared inside you as a ball of pulsing blood, or simply as redness in color, producing vibratory heat and filling your torso. Or imagine you're in the presence of someone's suffering, and instead of noticing your "compassion" in the form of a word in your mind, you find a soft brick sitting inside your upper chest cavity, glowing emerald green, tender to the touch and bringing tears to your eyes.

The thousands of people who have encountered one or more of these distinct body-forms describe them as emerging from a subtle space but arriving with a distinct sense of their own truth and existence. They don't feel like imagination; they feel real.

The same people also say that these body-forms evoke feelings that are richer than vocabulary or typical mental concepts. Some people describe it as a sudden inrush of God, or a sense of a prayer being answered, or simply a stillness that fills them with a notion of well-being. Whatever it is, they know it is divine.

Chapter 2

The Big Five

I was introduced to the thirty-five body-forms one by one, over the course of several years. The first five, I was told, held a special place. They were fundamental needs that allow human beings to function and think. I learned them in order: *joy, strength, will, compassion,* and *power.* Some were fun to explore. I got a big kick out of my encounter with *joy.* But my first attempts to find *strength* and *will* inside were harrowing. I had long worried that I lacked internal strength and will, and facing the possibility that I had been right all along was terrifying. After I describe the five briefly, and how they interact, I'll devote more time to each. These, by the way, are the five that Ali connected to the Sufi *lataif* system.

Joy is shorthand for the beginning of anything new. It includes curiosity, spontaneity, and not-knowing. It's a bright feeling, usually appearing as canary yellow. It often accompanies a sudden feeling of *I want.*

Strength is shorthand for the feeling that something is achievable. It includes aggression, and it includes discrimination – the ability to closely define what needs analysis. It's a fierce or full-blooded feeling, appearing as ruby red. It often accompanies the feeling of *I can*.

Will is just what it sounds like. It's about standing tall, with confidence. It's a feeling of purpose and drive, appearing as silver or white. It often accompanies the feeling of *I will*.

Compassion is about being in the world as a human, and knowing suffering. It's a feeling of love, and specifically lovingkindness, appearing as emerald green. It often accompanies the feeling of *I am*.

Power is shorthand for a state of knowing completely. It includes peace, too. It's a feeling of being grounded and still, appearing as a deep black. It often accompanies the feeling of *I know*.

Think of these five as the basics of a personality. They comprise the primary traits that you need to be an active human. Like most people, I feel more at ease with some of my five capacities than others. The others need work and drive my feelings of inferiority. So if my concern is *will*, I'll label myself "lazy." If my concern is *strength*, I'll call myself "weak." Much of my personality develops from covering up my feelings of deficiency. My mix of strengths and deficiencies sits underneath my overall personality. For instance, depending on where I stand on *strength*, I might be the sort of person who cedes power quickly, or alternately who takes command. Depending on where I stand on *joy*, which contains curiosity, I might be the kind of person who is set in their ways, or the kind who takes lots of risks.

My guess is that a personality test could be drawn up for these five, and that the results could be mapped to profiling systems such as Myers-Briggs and the enneagram. This is the territory of Jungian archetypes, and can generate helpful tips for getting along with people in the familiar world. But there's much more here than a parlor game or team-building exercise. While this path opens up an understanding of your beliefs in your own deficiencies, its real power emerges as those beliefs – which cause much of the emotional conflict in life – are replaced with an appreciation of your inner supports.

Let's look more closely at how my sense of capacity and deficiency – in the case in point, willpower and laziness – affects my everyday life. For most people, suffering implies an emotional struggle. When I'm caught in an emotional conflict, whether as an internal debate or external fight, I think there's something wrong that I have to do something about. I think I need to tap my own capacities to fix what's wrong. If I'm feeling belittled by a martinet boss, I might seek out anger as a way to stand up to him. I feel it's up to me to set a strategy for overcoming an obstacle. As I enter the conflict, I tense up, or steel myself, or put on a face. Or perhaps I go the other way and withdraw from the conflict, and then turn my anger upon myself for giving up, yet again. In my mind, I may have egoic delusions of grandeur of how one day I will make him suffer, or I'll be the boss, or I'll die and he will feel sorry, etc.

In this way, we take our feelings of insecurity into the situation and cloak them with a false sense of strength. But who is it who feels insecure? I believe that it's my underlying being, my sense of self based on memories of past crushing miseries. This is the sense of self that requires defenses. As it happens, there are only three: anger, withdrawal, or grandiosity. We can yell. We can sulk. We can make up a story and pity our boss. Each is a way to protect our insecure ego. Imagine a life without needing anger, withdrawal, or grandiosity. That would require a sense of self without insecurity.

This book offers a new way to examine your ego's built-up stories and recognize that you don't need them. You think you are dark or insufficient, but discover that you are light and supported.

In my own case, I was led to examine my life in relation to the primary five body-forms. While I thought I was studying the body-forms, I was really examining my own insecurities. I explored my history of ease or uneasiness with each body-form – when did I turn off my *curiosity*, or relinquish my *strength*, for instance? I explored the related messages that my inner critic, or ego, was sending me. This was astonishing work to me. Instead of avoiding my deficiencies, or accepting them as set in stone, I jumped right into them as objects of curiosity. I spent time figuring out where they had first emerged, and how I was attacked by them.

Sometimes I had to laugh at the absurdity of it all. I remember testing my basic insecurity by walking a busy sidewalk, looking at all the passersby while chanting under my breath in a sing-song voice, "Nobody loves me. Nobody cares." I took to watching my compensatory strategies. And finally I considered what it would be like if I didn't have to fill the hole of the particular deficiency, and I recognized how much of my time, to say nothing of my suffering, was related to compensating for perceived but unproven deficiencies. When I didn't have to do that, I had time to look around and enjoy whatever was sitting right in front of me.

Each of the first five body-forms relates to a set of common beliefs of deficiency. As I studied a particular set, it would eventually open that divine body-form. Over the course of time, the divine forms of *joy, strength, will, power,* and *compassion* made themselves known. Over a longer period of time, as I pursued my false identities and examined them, one or another of the five would suddenly start me shaking, not so much outwardly as inwardly. I felt slightly dizzy when this happened. For a few of the body-forms, the shaking lasted a few minutes, for one or two it took hours. This later happened with other body-forms. I learned to treasure the shaking: It signaled that my body and soul were integrating that body-form, that essential aspect. I was rewiring my internal belief system. Old structures based on my concern for being deficient were breaking apart. Along with the integration of the true essence of *will,* or *joy,* or whichever aspect, came the permanently lodged lesson that I wasn't actually deficient in that way, and that even if I continued to feel that I was (and I did and I do at times, but far less so), I had access to a divine form of the capacity that would take care of things in the end.

This is emotional and spiritual alchemy. The idea of turning lead into gold is a metaphor for the very human process of working with a false leaden idea of how things work, and examining it long enough for it to turn into a bright, golden truth. It works like this: I think I need to make up for a deficiency. I do what all humans do. I produce a shadowy form of what I need – call it false joy or false strength or false will or false power or false compassion. I pump myself up. I coach myself. I search for a paradigm. It's false because it's a behavior that I learn by watching other people over time, a strategy to get past an obstacle. I don't believe that I have the capacity to do the thing by myself; I think I have to use somebody else's idea that has been taught me. Each time I run into the deficiency I have to go find my faking-it strategy. Even if things turn out OK, I can't really take credit, since I've decided beforehand that I'm deficient and need to fake it to make it.

But if I notice all of that going on, and I bother to pay attention to my sense of my deficiency, and take the time to explore it objectively, the door opens for the divine body-form to enter. Once I've seen the body-form enough times to believe it is a more stable presence in me, it rewires me, shaking things out of the way so that it can permanently lodge in an accessible place.

For me, now that I have been introduced to the five, now that I have spent time with them, worked on the underlying issues they relate to, and integrated them, they are available to me as a replacement for my having to fake it. It's a great blessing. They can be drawn on in many circumstances. I've had them arrive in quite trivial situations: Once I was in a seven-mile running race – nothing new, I'm a lifelong distance runner – but found myself suddenly losing steam up a steep hill. I still had half the race to go, and I had bonked. For some reason I knew to let go of trying to do anything about it, and out of nowhere I felt a rich, fluid redness suffuse my body, keeping me strong and relaxed all the way to the finish line. It wasn't a typical runner's high; it was an inborn support.

I've also had the five arrive in quite difficult situations. One morning recently I lost my will to write this book. Instead of my usual strategy of fighting myself, I let it go – let myself feel my own loss of will, and examined it as it whirled around and exposed dread and paralysis. The next thing I knew, my body went silver, and I approached my computer with a restored sense of lightness. I wish it were always so easy!

The colors of the five are particularly vivid to people. *Joy* is yellow, *strength* is red, *will* is white, *power* is black, and *compassion* is green.

While they may be the most common body-forms, the Big Five are of equal weight to the other thirty. They are like-sized facets of God, stored inside you. Each has the capacity to both show a quality of God and boost your own access to divinity. Some aspects might be more useful for you, and for another person others might be more useful, and appear more often. They mostly show up as needed. *Strength* will emerge in view if you need strength. So among the gifts of the body-forms is their everyday usefulness. But none of that matters for now. As you learn to evoke them, you'll experience their effect on you. It's different for everybody, because we're all in a different place of finding our true selves and true nature. Wherever you are, the divine body-forms will find you there.

Shapes of Truth

Chapter 3

The Body-Forms
Answer Our Prayers

Everybody's got their issues. You're scared of your boss. Your friend hates her mother-in-law. Your other friend is a pompous ass. Yet another is a shrinking violet. You're irritated by their issues, and fascinated too. Most gossip centers around issues – mine and yours and theirs. We talk endlessly about the annoyances, fears, and struggles we have in this complicated world living among strangers. It's hard to be human, for everyone.

A Buddhist might say, "By issues you mean what we call suffering. They're just illusion. Get rid of attachment to such illusion, and you'll stop suffering." A Christian might say, "By issues you mean separating people into enemies and friends. Stop doing that. Treat everyone as a friend." A Hindu might say, "By issues you mean the interests of the small self, who abides in a narrow world of self-interest. Find your big Self and abide in wonder." A Muslim might say, "By issues you mean being forgetful of the Law. Pray and chant your way back into the Law and join Allah." A psychologist might say, "By issues you mean the burden of your traumas. Heal your past, and feel autonomous."

You can call them issues, or illusions, misunderstandings, neuroses, conflicts, attachments, sufferings, miseries, defenses, shadows, fears, separations, self-talk, mortifications, or any of hundreds of incisive words that intend to hint at a way out of trouble. One name is as good as another for us here. We'll arbitrarily stick with "issues."

I'm going to propose a finite list of issues common to human beings, and that the total sum of issues numbers thirty-five. Here's my list. As you go through them, circle five that particularly apply to yourself.

It's not safe. I'm stupid. I'm childish. I'm angry. I doubt myself. I don't know what to believe. The world lets me down. I'm unlovable. I want my mom to take care of me. I want my dad to take care of me. I am separated from love. I am guilty. I've been rejected. I need to resist. My feelings are hurt. I need that. I need to be liked. I don't belong here. I need to get along with my life. I'm worthless. Other people are full of it. It's a dog-eat-dog world. All I am is a body with a brain. I have to go along to get along. I'm always defending myself. There's no heaven here on earth. I'm sensitive to conditions. I need to be seen and known. I'm too self-centered. I don't like my body. Things are never quite right. I'm rigid. I need to achieve more. I'm scared of death. I lose myself on autopilot. More selflessness would be impractical.

I'll bet you've experienced most of these at some time or another. They may all lurk, waiting for the right occasion to spring forward.

Your five are not my five. They could be, and I can relate to your five, but the odds are that I'll circle some that you don't. We all have our own personalities, interests, primary issues, and fears. One way to look at our variety as individual human beings is to see the incredible number of possibilities that can be created by mixing and matching within this simple list of thirty-five common issues. Yes, we can be defined by our talents and masteries, but we can be defined equally by our miseries and defenses. Just ask your partners or children, who have seen you at your worst and most despairing. They may know your issues better than you do.

If you've got an issue that doesn't appear on the list, find the closest approximation. But don't be concerned that you don't have your five down pat. It doesn't matter. You'll have a chance to investigate all thirty-five, if you want. And if you decide to just investigate a random one or two, that'll be enough, too. This is as open-ended exploration as you want it to be.

Here's where these thirty-five issues take you:

Each one is a shadow form of a divine body-form. Each issue connects directly to one of the thirty-five, inborn divine body-forms. By inborn, I mean literally inside you, already. You may have fought the issue through books and therapists, and crying on the shoulders of loved ones. You may have confronted the issue with strategies, or workarounds, or denial or acceptance. I'm offering you one more chance at conquering the issue. It is my belief that you have a tool inside you designed to address that very issue. The tool is the divine body-form that corresponds to that very issue of yours. Here's how it seems to work:

Let's say your issue is contained in the thought "I'm worthless." This is very common. It might be an upfront belief, where you have consistently low self-esteem. Or it might be hidden in a subliminal layer that mutters that if you don't do something about it, people will notice how worthless you are. Or it might just show up occasionally, as a fleeting concern that you bring no particular value to the world. Strong or weak in its belittling voice, the feeling of having little worth is dependent on the idea that value is externally determined. Your value is measured by your achievements, or your relative power or fame or riches, or your ability to turn people's heads. The idea might be that if you did nothing of value to others, you would be a blob, so worthless that you would be rejected and abandoned to die. If so, all of your value rests in what you bring to the world or show of your abilities. If value is only externally derived, you have to keep working, keep being productive, keep showing your abilities, in order to retain your value. If your ranking slips, through losing fame or power or riches or simply by aging, your whole being and purpose declines with it. This, by the way, is the standard model that civilization establishes for us.

Have you ever wondered why billionaires don't stop when they reach a lower but still fantastic amount of wealth and relax into a life of ease? (Personally I would quit at ten million plus a fund for the permanent upkeep of a 75-foot yacht.) It's that the fear of worthlessness drives their exaggerated ambitions, and the piled-up money never succeeds in overcoming the fear. Their worth is tied up in their relative ranking of wealth. If it drops, so does their sense of self; they're on a hamster wheel of more, more, more. No self-made billionaire got there by accident or by virtue. They got there by negative self-worth, often well-hidden.

Now I'm going to introduce you to a concept that might be difficult to accept: intrinsic self-worth. Imagine for a moment that value wasn't externally derived. Imagine that you weren't an empty vessel, ready to fill itself up with the right stuff that reflected society's rankings. Imagine instead that you have a permanent reservoir of value that you were born with, which can neither be added to nor reduced by the outside world. Your intrinsic value is the exact same size and weight as anyone else's, too. No one has more value, no one less. Having intrinsic value is quite ordinary, and requires no upkeep. It's permanent, stable, and travels with you wherever you go.

This is extremely hard to believe. In a sense, this is what Jesus kept trying to knock into the apostles' heads. "Guys, you're just like everyone else. You are everyone else. No one's better or worse. Quit ranking people. Quit calling some friends, others enemies. You're more alike than you think. And by the way, you partake of the divine."

If I am a divine being, how in the world could I lack value?

Like I said, this is incredibly difficult to believe.

So my body offers me a way to believe it. It offers me a divine body-form. The body-form isn't intrinsic value itself. It's a liminal experience that takes me to the cutting edge where reality meets imagination. The body-forms are in a way metaphoric, while at the same time palpable and real. Later in the book, I'll show you how to elicit body-forms yourself, in your own body. But we need to get a clearer understanding of what they are first, and that includes what they look like.

Encountering a body-form is a specific experience, the same for anyone. The appearance of any one body-form is the same for me or for you. If it's a vocabulary of thirty-five representations, then we are all born with the same vocabulary. We'll use the body-form of intrinsic value as the example here.

In your chair, close your eyes and use your imagination to look inside your torso. It's probably full of ribs and organs and pumping and blood and arteries and veins and all sorts of things, with very little empty space. Obviously you can't actually see all that. You don't have X-ray vision. But you can use your mind, memory, and senses to imagine the different parts in their different places.

Now imagine that a transparent six-inch cube with rounded corners is scooped out in the middle of your torso. You've been hollowed out. The organs and bones and other physical parts in that area have been moved out of the way. You don't notice where; they're just gone. There's an empty hollow in your torso. Then something appears in it, as if in a snow-globe. In this case, what appears is a walnut-sized irregular piece of amber. It looks just like a real piece of amber, but it's sitting in your torso, glowing yellow-orange and offering its mysterious smoky interior to your sight. Its color transfixes you as a piece of amber in a store might. But it's within you, within the transparent cube in your torso, in plain sight.

There you have it. That's what it's like to encounter a body-form. It's that simple and that unusual. It lasts a few minutes, and then the hollow closes up. Your eyes open and the world returns to normal.

That's the basic experience of the body-form. There are variations. Often the hollow won't reveal a solid object, but will turn the color of the object. Each of the thirty-five divine body-forms has its own color. Sometimes multiple body-forms will appear at once, or in quick succession, or an object will change color and become a different body-form. Some of the body-forms may come with scents or tastes or densities of their own. If they do, any other person going inside who comes across that scent or taste is experiencing that exact same body-form with the same meaning and purpose.

Each of the body-forms has a meaning, as a characteristic of the divine. The purpose, as you will see, is to address that particular issue you have, and show you that hidden inside you is the support for moving past that issue into freedom from it. If my value is intrinsic, and I come to believe that, then my sense of default worthlessness disappears, and maybe my need to spend time measuring myself against others can relax or even go away.

This is so hard to believe that we'll go into detail about some of the thirty-five issues and their corresponding divine body-forms. By reading a number of examples, you'll start to get used to the conceptual framework that turns a peculiar experience into a healing program. You can go through them all or pick out a few that seem particularly relevant to your life. After that, we'll discuss the simple technique to reveal the divine body-forms inside you. In the meantime, here's a list of all the issues and their corresponding divine body-forms.

Joy/Curiosity	I'm not safe.
Strength	I'm stupid.
Will	I'm childish.
Compassion	I'm angry.
Power	I doubt myself.
Truth	I don't know what to believe.
Trust	The world lets me down.
Personal love	I'm unlovable.
Merging love	I want my mom to take care of me.
Passionate love	I want my dad to take care of me.
Universal love	I'm separated.
Forgiveness	I'm guilty.

Acceptance	I've been rejected.
Surrender	I need to resist.
Vulnerability	My feelings are hurt.
Gratitude	It has to be mine.
The Point	I need to be liked.
The Pearl	I don't belong here.
Brilliancy	I need to get along with my life.
Value	I'm worthless.
Knowingness	Other people's beliefs are nonsense.
Universal will	It's a dog-eat-dog world.
Existence	I'm just a body with a brain.
Sincerity	I have to go along to get along.
Melting	I'm always defending myself.
Spirituality	There's no heaven here on earth.
Contentment	I'm sensitive to conditions.
Impersonality	I need to be seen and known.
Nourishment	I'm too self-centered.
Space	I don't like my body.
Satisfaction	Things are never quite right.
Clear	I'm rigid.
Fulfillment	I need to achieve more.
Death Space	I'm scared of death.
Impeccability	I lose myself on autopilot.
Anointment	I'm selfless enough already.

As you follow along through the examples, ask whether the body-forms you meet might help transform your collection of personal issues – the pesky parts of your life that keep you small – into a garden of delights that hold dear your big, expansive, and divine self.

Shapes of Truth

Chapter 4

❧

Joy/
Curiosity

As little kids in the Fifties and Sixties, many of us shared the dream of running away to join the circus. Its strange big-top world stretched far outside our tame little lives into lions and stilt-walkers and trick riding and acrobats. One of my few regrets is that when I got the chance to join the circus, I choked.

I was 18 and my life was a wreck. I had returned from my childhood home in Arlington, Virginia, to Santa Fe, New Mexico for my sophomore year of college. Two weeks in, I gave up. My intention had been to take school more seriously, but I was partying harder than ever. In fact, I had shown up on campus on the acid that I got from a woman I met on the train to New Mexico. Things declined from there. A couple of my friends were in similar shape, or so they said. We hatched a plan. We would drop out, head to

India and walk the hippie mysticism trail, following in the footsteps of the Beatles and Ram Dass and Allen Ginsberg. One of us, Hunter, was wealthy and would pay for our flights from the East Coast, where the other two of us would meet him in two weeks. So John and I set out to hitchhike across the country from Santa Fe to Boston.

Around midnight outside Amarillo, John bailed. In the haunting lights of the overpass in the middle of nowhere, I watched him cross the interstate, wave one more time, face east and stick his thumb out to westbound traffic. I resumed facing the opposite direction, and a ride showed up as a middle-aged guy in a Mercedes who took me a couple of exits. Then a semi- driver who was bugged out and talkative on speed took me all the way to Oklahoma City, where sleepless I hooked up with another hippie vagabond, a roughed-up version of the surfer type, who had been on the road for several years. A few hundred miles along we were hungry, and my new friend Derek showed me how to shoplift sandwiches from a convenience store, so we ate by the side of the highway before getting a final ride that landed us on the outskirts of Little Rock, Arkansas, one late afternoon.

We trudged off the interstate, looking around for a place to unroll our sleeping bags and pitch camp for the night. Both of us were exhausted. Derek stopped and studied a placard stapled to a utility pole.

"What's today?" he asked.

"I don't know, Sunday?"

"I mean what's the date?"

"Oh, I think the 16th."

"Come on, we can get some work."

Itinerants know the ways of other itinerants, it turns out. The placard was for a traveling carnival that had spent the previous week lit up and busy on a vacant lot in Little

Rock. The poster had informed Derek that today was its last day in town. Sure enough, when we got to the spot, around six, roustabouts were at work disassembling the booths and rides. It was a big carnival that besides the midway included a menagerie and freak show. Derek got the two of us hired on as hands. I helped break down the carousel, for $2 an hour.

Six hours later, the foreman counted out twelve singles and said, "You're a good worker. If you want, you can join us. You'll share a berth on the train over there. We're heading south in an hour or so, a few weeks more of stops, and then there's more work when we winter in Florida."

The half-dozen train cars hummed at the edge of the lot, their windows glowing yellow and inviting, and then I happened to glance to my right, where much closer, across the street, a motel's neon sign lit up a painted board that said $12/NITE. When I woke the next morning, thinking clearly from a night of sleep, I banged my head against the motel room wall. I had been invited to join the circus, and I had refused.

I didn't get to India for nearly forty years. I instead thumbed the rest of the way to my parents' house and called Hunter and told him that India was off for me. I cut my hair and took a job as a bank teller.

We all have our limits. I'm pretty risk-tolerant. Taking LSD with a stranger, dropping out of school on a whim, hitchhiking, shoplifting, heading to India. I kept my eyes open and my curiosity brimming. But tired and dirty, I found my limits. Interestingly, of all the risks I took in the story, the only one that might have paid off in a substantial way – experiencing life as a carney for a season or two – was the one I refused. Was it that I wasn't clear-minded, or that it was too weird? My curiosity succumbed to the offer of a soft mattress.

I Need to Be More Careful

We all have our limits. What's the biggest risk you took? How did it turn out?

Taking risks – getting out of our comfort zones – is rooted in curiosity. In a way, it is what curiosity is all about. Curiosity is the exploration of what is right around us, and the hardest part of that work is to see what's on the other side of the typical boundaries.

Many of us had parents who discouraged too much curiosity. Testing the limits can feel like its own taboo. If I grew up poor, I was likely to be channeled into a safe trade. "Stop that writing nonsense. Take accounting classes, or programming." Other messages were drilled in: Don't question authority. Play by the rules. Better safe than sorry. Curiosity killed the cat.

When curiosity is curtailed, it's called living within the boundaries, coloring within the lines, and playing it safe. The idea is that boundaries are sacrosanct, the rules are most important, and we need to listen to others to find out what is safe for us. All of this is true on the survival side of life: My skin must be protected from injury, snake venom kills, and stoves burn. But how true is it on the other side of life? If you're a serious rule-follower, don't you notice the playful rule-breakers seem to be having fun? What if they're also living an appropriate life? Is that open to you as an idea?

I have a voice inside me that tells me when I'm about to go too far. It's called a conscience. Psychologists call it my superego. It's a storehouse for social rules. It includes rules like the Ten Commandments, and others like the

Constitution and the driver's manual. It includes the serious, frowning side of my parental figures. It steps in when I'm about to be too playful and scolds me back to grim reality. "Behave yourself," it says.

What if I wish I could occasionally color outside the lines, or travel to a far city without feeling scared? Think about it. No matter how restrained you may be, how risk-averse, incurious, or safety-conscious, I'll bet there have been times you wished you could be a little more adventurous, like that wild friend of yours.

Pure Curiosity as a Concept

First let's see what's true about pure curiosity that might be different from the commonplace, questionable kind that has safety as its opposite.

Pure curiosity is around far more often than you might think. Every moment, experience, complete thought, plan, strategy, scheme, and event begins with curiosity. Curiosity is the simple task of looking around and seeing what you've got on hand. It's how everything starts for you, for me, for everyone. The arc of a moment, an experience, a thought, or a strategy has a beginning of curiosity, a middle of activity, and an end of meaning.

Curiosity asks, "What's here?" If I'm climbing a mountain, at the top I stop and look around. Before I get to the idea "That's beautiful," I've looked and looked, cataloguing the things I see in the panorama. That cataloguing is curiosity. If I'm planning a garden, I study the soil, the elevation, the availability of sun and water, the possible plants, the aesthetics, and the pests, among other variables, and assemble them all into my scope before I start the plant selection and sorting process.

To a baby, curiosity is the simple act of taking something from near proximity and drawing it closer for inspection. A baby doesn't know what a "ball" is. It sees a close-by protuberance and draws it into its mouth, to investigate. All curiosity is like that. Curiosity is what tells us what things are, and how available they are. When in our curiosity, we scan the wide view and pluck out the things that may be of interest.

Oddly, this is described by the words "I want." It turns out that wanting something is the same as pulling it closer for investigation and possible use. We take something out of the far or middle distance – say an ice cream cone, which we pull from the counter of a shop. When it hits our mouth, we have begun our investigation, no differently than when we were infants.

As adults, the objects of curiosity – the possible nearby variables to combine and test – include abstract concepts and human constructions (for instance, I might test what is "honesty" or "God") as well as concrete objects like bouncy balls and mashed peas. So we draw possible variables from our stored memories – some of them metaphors and some of them as fixed and concrete as mathematical equations, some vague and others already well parsed – and throw them into the mix.

If I'm asking what is God, in a way I'm pulling God closer, for investigation. If I'm asking whether to take a risk, I'm pulling it closer for investigation. One trick is to notice that there's no danger in wanting something, in pulling it closer in your imagination. Curiosity didn't kill the cat. Stalking did. She had to run toward her object of desire. I can want an ice cream cone and not get it. My constraint might save me calories. Peril only arrives when I have an expectation of *getting* what I want. Then I'm in trouble, every which way. So don't deprive yourself of wanting anything or everything, or of being more curious. Just be realistic; you're not going to get most of what you want, and the part you do get probably won't turn out to be exactly what you expected.

The Bridge

How do I make curiosity more my friend? I don't want to be reckless or dangerous. But maybe I'm a little rigid, a little stuck in my ways. Am I cutting off my curiosity too soon?

If you ever ask these questions, then finding access to pure curiosity, one of the divine body-forms, might be fun. Do you have a firehose of playful curiosity tucked away somewhere, hiding from you and waiting to be released? If you do, then the divine body-form can act as a bridge to take you to where you want to go.

The Body-Form of Curiosity

What is curiosity as a body-form? Like all body-forms, it shows up in a surprising opening in your body. In part of your body, usually inside your head or torso, some organs get pushed aside to leave a hollow – the snow-globe – where the body-form can express itself. It's like something out of your imagination, but when you look in at it, it feels real.

Mostly you'll see the color yellow, in its pure, primary color form. It may or may not be attached to an imaginary object inside. It might just be a color suffused into the air or mist that is filling the hollow. It has a feeling, too, that you might sense the way you can feel liquid in your throat by swallowing. The palpable sensation of curiosity inside is effervescent. Clients of mine describe bubbles rising through their body. You can feel the bubbles moving up in gentle streams, as if your belly is a giant glass of mysteriously light champagne. The whole interior of the torso can turn yellow, or there might be little yellow specks in a field of another color. I have experienced it as a yellow stripe accompanying a series of changing events. It has a lightness of being, and can erupt in joy and literally bring a smile to your face. In fact, the word joy represents a feeling that accompanies this pure form of curiosity all the time. It's as if joy is the same thing as curiosity, just on another level. Things that are new, surprising, unusual, or unexpected bring us joy; you might notice joy in everyday curiosity, too.

Inside your torso or head, the pure body-form of curiosity may be the main subject of an experience, or it might be a color that is one of several in an experience. It may stick around for a while, or disappear quickly. As it continues to draw your attention, its purity will be evident, and if you check how you feel overall, even away from the bubbly presence in your torso, you might notice a simpler feeling of contentment.

Generally you'll get at most five or ten minutes of a divine body-form, just enough to believe that it happened to you. That's its medicine. You get one dose at a time. But over a succession of encounters, you might notice the yellow showing up again, and again. Somehow, by the tenth or so time you have seen it, its support will rewire your beliefs. You'll come to the understanding that *curiosity* isn't dangerous, even if expectation of *getting* is.

So far the bridge has taken you in one direction, from your worry that you're too rigid about some things to noticing that you have a capacity for pure curiosity, and that it's divine and not dangerous or reckless. Now your job is to reverse course and cross back over the same bridge into your regular life. When you do, you might no longer fear curiosity as a danger, but instead see it as a dependable support. If you've got the support of curiosity within you, and it's not dangerous, how safe might it be to open it up in your daily life? It's not that you'll go out and start hitchhiking around the country; you'll be in your same life, doing your usual things, but you'll be more open to listening to the other side, and more interested in the edges of things. Simply put, curiosity won't seem like a perilous temptation. It may be as safe as a drive in the country.

Curiosity is worth knowing. It is playful, open, and joyful. If you get to know it, and notice that it is suspended at the beginning of everything, it will amplify itself in your everyday life. That's the alchemy of the body-forms.

Shapes of Truth

Chapter 5

✌ ❧

Strength

The following year I returned to school in Santa Fe. I buckled down, and schoolwork seemed much easier and enjoyable. I kept my head above water in my philosophy, music, geometry, and biology classes. Language class was another matter. Two years of Greek were required, and while I had somehow faked my way through my first year as a freshman, my sophomore professor wasn't easily fooled. She forced my ignorance into the open, and I collapsed. Instead of seeking help, starting over and painstakingly moving through the early lessons to eventually catch up, I decided I was incapable of learning Greek. Eventually I concluded that my problem wasn't that I had not taken it seriously from the start; it was an inborn inability to memorize. I recalled the earlier shame of dropping lines in childhood theater productions. I linked my Greek failure to the Cs and Ds I got in higher math in high school. I was sure that I was a bright enough guy in some ways, but my brain lacked the capacity for dependable memorization.

My sophomore Greek teacher wanted to kick me out of school. Fortunately, my other professors came to my rescue. My Greek teacher was shocked to learn from them that I wasn't necessarily a lazy bastard, but seemed to have some hang-up about her class. Seething, she was forced to tolerate me for the rest of the year. I felt ashamed, guilty, and also proud that I had put one over on her. She became the enemy. Contempt toward the shamer can be an effective self-defense.

But in a sense, she won. Ever since, I have made sure to hide my memorization deficiency.

I'm Stupid

We all have a sense of limits to our capacity to learn or do. We rank ourselves and each other on how smart we are and how strong we are. Are you capable of something? If yes, you're OK. If no, you're deficient, which is not OK. This concern can take many forms. Have you ever thought or said to yourself any of these kinds of statements:

- I can't hold up my end.
- I can't carry the weight.
- I'm so dumb, so stupid.
- That was so dumb of me.
- I'm a fraud and everyone knows it.
- My knowledge is only skin deep.
- Other people are so much better at this.
- They know the secret rules.
- No one takes me seriously, and why should they?

> ❧ They look at me like I'm an idiot.

> ❧ I don't get it, and I'm pretty sure I can't get it.

All of these statements question your capacity to figure things out. Whether you rest in your sense of deficiency frequently or occasionally, recognize that it's a universal ailment. Everybody has the same kind of self-talk.

Pure Strength as a Concept

Strength covers the sum total of your inner and outer capacities. Your sense of strength represents your comfort or discomfort with saying, "I can."

It turns out that most opportunities to express strength are not physical. Most daily experiences and tasks are more about figuring things out than about lifting, hauling, or pushing physical objects around. And you need strength – the sense that you *can do* something – in all of your thoughtful, emotional, and productive endeavors. Once you recognize that, you might want to use a more refined synonym for strength, the word "discrimination," as in "discernment" or "distinction." When you *discriminate* things accurately, you're sorting the world into its useful *parts* and using your skills to reassemble them to complete your task.

Let's imagine that life is a series of puzzles. Sometimes the world gives me a puzzle to solve – a new task, a new conflict with my partner, a new desire that seeks fulfillment – and other times I give myself a puzzle – a new goal, a new choice of study, a new self-improvement plan.

The first thing I do with a puzzle is look around and see what I have to work with. I lay all the pieces out on the table. We covered that step in the chapter on *curiosity*. Now I've got all my pieces or variables picked out, and it's time to play with them and see how they work together to achieve a solution to the task or puzzle. That's *discrimination.* I'm bearing down on how they fit together, like pieces in a puzzle, to efficiently help me to my goal, the solution to the puzzle or the completion of the task. If I have guessed well in the first round, the curiosity part at the beginning, the pieces will be just what I need to get to my goal. But we're eighty percenters, us humans. In anything we do, we get it wrong an embarrassing amount of the time. That's because things are always changing up on us, becoming slightly different from before. *Discrimination* helps us see what needs refinement, so that the twenty percent we got wrong can be thoughtfully removed and replaced by something else. *Discrimination* is like applied science; we analyze – which takes one thing and breaks it into components – or we synthesize – which takes two things and combines them into a new thing. The more accurately we perform these functions, the more efficient we are in solving the puzzle or completing the task. In this respect, we're all smart as hell. We just have our respective masteries. In our masteries – with a lathe, or a pen, or a trumpet, or a spreadsheet, or a manifold, or a rake – we're using our training to *discriminate* among the variables in front of us better than the average bear.

Think of Muhammad Ali. As a boxer, he wasn't the most musclebound. But he had enough power to knock out Sonny Liston quickly. And he had an advantage over many of his opponents. His rope-a-dope dancing around – not offering a stable target until he was ready to box – gave him time to study how his opponent reacted to being off-balance, study his reflexes when confused or overwhelmed, and otherwise just record some useful information before getting into the battle. While he could box superbly, Ali didn't win with musclebound strength; he won with his superior ability to *discriminate* what his opponent was up to and mix up his big blows with clever, off-putting cuts and jabs. He's considered the greatest of all time by most boxing critics because he could do it all, and a lot of it was brains.

Ali knew he was strong. Most of us worry that we're not strong enough. That can take two forms: the myth of the 98-pound weakling, and the myth of the blockhead. In the myth of the 98-pound weakling, you're inferior to others because you suck at field hockey or baseball. In the myth of the blockhead, you're inferior to others because you suck at math or reading. With little evidence usually, you have decided that you don't have as much capacity as others. So what do you do? You fake it. You stay away from experiences that might expose your self-defined weaknesses.

I'm sure that you're convinced that you've been held back in some ways by your deficiencies. Everybody tells that self-referential lie. I'm not going to argue with you on that one. I'm just asking you to allow in the possibility – just for a few minutes – that you might have all the discriminatory power, the strength, that you need inside waiting to be noticed, accepted, and tapped. This isn't wishful thinking. It's just that you need a lot less strength than you thought. Muhammad Ali chose a course of life in which he needed to develop certain forms of physical and mental strength, and he did so and found a mastery that let him ease into life. That was his path. Yours isn't his. If you're an adult over twenty-five reading this book, you've probably already been channeled into the mastery that will continue to ease your way through life. Now that you're there, the body-form of strength can help you along wherever your mastery might take you. The point isn't to be the best or greatest. The point is for it to be enough to make life easy. Finding the divine form of strength inside you might convince you of this.

The Bridge

Suffering through this sense of deficiency, you might ask, "How can I feel more confident that I'm smart enough, strong enough, or capable enough? Do I need to go back to school, build up my muscles, or apply more effort? Or might my relentless claim that I'm fundamentally deficient be self-fulfilling? I've tried changing my attitude, and my feeling of weakness eventually returns, always."

But think about it. What you've left out from all your prior considerations is the possibility that you might be wrong. What if feeling stupid is a misunderstanding? What if you're not stupid or weak or incapable? What would that look like?

The willingness to question your most basic notion of deficiency is the bridge to finding your innate strength and capacity. If you can find your way past your sense of deficiency, you can discover the pure strength that abides within you.

The Body-Form of Pure Strength

What is strength or discrimination as a body-form? Like all body-forms, it shows up in an opening in your torso or neck. Just like with curiosity, organs get pushed aside to leave an empty, transparent spot where the body-form can be revealed. You're using your visual imagination, but the result is a palpable, if foreign, experience.

Real strength doesn't have to be faked, summoned, or secured from the outside. It resides within. In its pure body-form, you might first find it in the heart region, spanning much of the area behind your sternum. If during an interior torso exploration you notice any red, you can be pretty sure that you're seeing divine *strength*, presenting itself as a personal asset. It's a kind of confidence that can't be broken or questioned.

Mostly you'll see the color red, as shiny and rich as a ruby. It may or may not be attached to an imaginary object inside. You might see an actual ruby, showing up like the piece of amber for the body-form of value. Or it might just be the color red suffused into the air or mist that is filling the hollow. It has a feeling, too; pure strength inside feels like pumping blood. Your heart center might push out, or pulse. You'll probably have a feeling of thick, rich aliveness. The whole interior of the torso can turn red, or there might be a red coating to another object inside.

The red experience, which may be isolated to a small object or may extend throughout your body, can stick around or disappear quickly. As it continues to draw your attention, its purity will be evident, and if you monitor how you feel overall, even away from its energetic presence in your torso, you might notice a simpler feeling of contentment.

Generally you'll get at most five or ten minutes of pure strength. But wow, what a five minutes! Suddenly being capable *enough* – to use your masteries to ease through life – may be enough for you. Let someone else win the Nobel Prize for physics.

So far the bridge has taken you in one direction, from your worry that you're incapable to the belief that you have strength inside, and that it's divine and not fake or insufficient. Now cross back over the bridge into your regular life. Can you notice that you have a dependable reservoir of strength inside?

Strength is worth knowing. It is full-blooded, confident, and even courageous. If you get to know its presence in the middle of any activity, it can help you along through the hard parts. That's the alchemy of the body-forms.

Chapter 6

Will

Forty-seven years after giving up on Greek, having proven incapable of rote, memorized learning, I took up Sanskrit. If this strikes you as imbecilic of me, I can muster no defense. But it wasn't masochism. Sanskrit was simply a required course for a program in Eastern Classics that I undertook. The rest of the program was mostly talking about old books, which I'm fine with. For the sake of the readings, I accepted the punishment of learning Sanskrit. It was one of those nasty unintended consequences, the persistent gremlins of life.

My wife had no idea what had hit her. Here we were, relaxing into the interior months of the pandemic in late summer, our lives cleared of busyness and enjoying isolation and its general reduction in family drama, sweetly spending evenings together viewing Scandinavian and British detective shows, when I had to muck it up with Sanskrit.

As I tackled the alphabet – 49 unfamiliar letters, many with unpronounceable sounds – my heart sank. All the old feelings that I lacked capacity returned. I looked up my nemesis Greek professor on Google, maybe to let her know I could still get the best of her. Instead I descended into the shame of holding in contempt someone who was now dead. Wandering around the house, muttering and scared, my suffering was on display hour after hour. At the root of my fear: Not only would I fail at this, everyone else in class would succeed.

Doomed, I applied myself. Hopeless, I attacked the alphabet. I kept a copy tucked into my back pocket, to be pulled out during daily walks. Several times a day I drilled myself with flash cards. I imagined my classmates as little Ronald Reagans, able to read a script once and know it forever. Me, I had to dumbly repeat these stupid sounds over and over and over again, only to lose them overnight and start again. Worst of all, I shut myself into my office many evenings, forcing my wife into reality TV on the nights I wasn't available for our shared detective shows. It was around then that Annie learned from her friend who leads Hindu sacred chanting sessions that there were four pronunciations in Sanskrit for the sound we know as "T," and she met me daily in our increasingly rare encounters in the kitchen and bedroom and living room with a mocking refrain of "tuh- tha- dtuh- dtha-."

Before the alphabet had a chance to sink in, we were on to the horror of declensions, in which a single noun or adjective has, instead of the one spelling that God gave it, up to seventy-two possibilities. And if you were to get one wrong, a Sanskrit-speaking child of ten would snicker behind your back. My living hell descended two or three rings. Now several weeks into the project, I veered from the worry that I couldn't succeed and took up the related but separate worry that I wouldn't persevere long enough to succeed.

It turned out that by diligently committing myself to memorizing Sanskrit for a couple of weeks, I had discovered that I had the capacity to do it. The alphabet got easier. But before that had sunk in, the second and equal fear – that I *wouldn't keep doing it* – took its place. This is the fear of being lazy, spineless, and childish. It's the fear that I didn't have enough willpower to get through the difficult parts of life, even the ones like Sanskrit that I had sort of volunteered for.

I Need to Grow Up

The fear of lacking will or steadfastness is tied to a more haunting feeling that you might not be fully grown up. Most of us feel this way sometimes. We might associate adulthood with serious activities and with grim hours finishing difficult tasks, leaving playfulness and fun activities to children. This Puritanical separation of work and play heightens the challenge to spend time in work, when what we so long for is simple fun.

My sense of being sapped of will takes many guises. Maybe you've heard about one or two of them: I'm lazy. I procrastinate. I put it off because I'm distractable, because I'm impulsive, because I'm a dope. If it was up to me, nothing would get done. Why do I need to steel myself just to do the dishes? I'm spineless. Why don't I stand up for myself? Somehow I feel neutered by these other people in the room. If I had more willpower, I could achieve great things, or at least keep my room tidy.

We have all the intention in the world at the start of a project. The energy of strength fills us. We're ready to tackle the world and have fun doing it. My task today is to clear out the storage shed around back. I've been meaning to do it for years. I could use the space, and if I haven't opened those boxes since we moved here, there's no point in keeping them. Should take no more than two hours, plus one or two dump runs. I have a pretty free weekend, and I'll feel good when I'm done. I march out to the shed. And then, even before I've opened the first box, a question shows up and I sit down to think. What if the dusty boxes in the storage shed turn out to be worth saving? I've got to sort through them and figure out which go to my grown kids and which stay here. How will I get this stuff to my grown children during the pandemic? Do I have to buy shipping boxes? Now instead of sorting through the junk in the shed, I'm sitting outside it, worrying and overwhelmed. In a way, I've already given up once. I'll have to pump myself up and start over again.

What happened? It's actually pretty simple. I ran into the unknown. In any project, I'm going to hit an unexpected consequence of my actions or thoughts. Some of those disturbances correct themselves easily. Others take me down rabbit holes. They're only troubling, though, because their bottom is not clear to me. How easy would it be to call an adult child and ask for help in sorting, at least by phone? What about taking the time to get some empty boxes before starting the sort?

Most stopping points that take the momentum out of a project are like that. They're easily repaired with a phone call to an expert or a small side project to arrange things. Consider whether your procrastination begins when you hit a hiccup, and whether the typical hiccup is such a big deal. But instead of noticing that it's just a hiccup, I look around and call myself a procrastinator. I belittle myself with the idea that I'm giving up because I'm lazy.

What would it feel like to be more steadfast, less prone to giving up early?

Pure Will as a Concept

Strength and will are companions. Strength says "I can do it." Will, true to its name, says "I will do it." It takes on the task and carries it out to completion. *Pure* will, which resides inside you, removes the emotional burden of feeling lazy, or immature, or spineless. It grants you fortitude and perseverance as if they're easy to find and use.

You have a lot more maturity and perseverance than you think. Notice for a moment that you get just about everything done. You recall the panicky times when you're rushing to meet a deadline, but you ignore all the other things you completed on the way. Notice how incredibly complicated your day is. You've focused on the one project that isn't getting done, but I'll bet just about everything else is. Asked how they procrastinate, most people talk about how they use the so-called interim to tidy their house, get the shopping done, return phone calls, or mow the lawn.

"I know I'm procrastinating when my desk is clear," one client told me. Think about that a moment. Those of you who put off big projects by completing little cleaning tasks know what she was talking about. Was she actually *procrastinating* by arranging neat piles on her desk, or wasn't she instead simply shuffling her responsibilities, and getting another task done first? She was still being productive, so why didn't she allow herself the right to have that choice, doing task B before task A? As participants in a complicated, industrialized society, we are incredibly busy human beings, probably among the most productive ever. Maintaining all of our belongings is practically a full-time job itself. If you're like most people, you don't give yourself any credit for the so-called small jobs, even if they add up to many hours a week.

"Well, they're simple, so I get them over with," my client told me.

Much of the trick to find steadfast progress in major, complicated tasks is noticing how they break down into smaller parts that can be handled one by one. Engineers are trained to do this. They have flow charts that include checkpoints to review how things are going. The bite-sized view keeps a programmer or mechanical engineer from being overwhelmed by a many-week goal. The other key to stopping yourself from getting freaked out and shutting down is to recognize that when you find yourself resisting the work, you've probably hit a limit to your abilities. You can still finish the project; you wouldn't have taken it on if it wasn't doable. You just need help from the outside. Every time I find myself hung up on a project, I look around for help. I didn't used to. I thought being resourceful meant doing it myself. It doesn't. It means making a phone call or, God forbid, asking for advice. (And nowadays, we have Google-ji to come to the rescue.)

Part of acquiring a sense of will is noticing that it's not your job alone to straighten your spine, that the world will help you up when you fall or when you're about to fail. Knowing this at the point of procrastination can reduce the time spent fretting and get the job completed faster.

Another characteristic of will is that it aims toward a goal. Sometimes the goal itself can be scary. Maybe I bit off more than I can chew. In the Tao Te Ching, Lao Tzu writes, "Failure usually happens on the verge of success." (This kind of self-sabotage often arrives when you don't notice that the quality of the final achievement is baked in way before the last steps are finished. Knowing that most of the work that matters is behind you can lead to a sense that the only point of the project is completion, not its reception in the world. The reception is already determined. Now your only task is to get it out there.)

Procrastination can feel like a loss of nerve. What might help here is to notice that the main point of finishing a project is simply to finish the project. It's not to accomplish something, or be respected, or get a good grade, although all those achievements are possible. It's mainly to complete it, so you can do the next thing. We complete things to shed them and make room for a new thing to do. Whether a project is embarked on for pay or for virtue or for glory or just fun, by the time you're at the end, all of that has already been settled. You set your expectations of quality at the beginning, and the actual quality has been mostly determined long before the last nail is pounded. The project ends, and it's time to move to the next thing to do, which might be lying around and basking in your freedom. Without feeling lazy, that is, at least for twenty-four hours.

There's only one class of people I know who don't commit to challenging projects. Old people. They've learned to put life on cruise control, and also to brake on occasion, get out, and smell the purple sage by the highway. But before coming to those realizations you're going to challenge yourself, and you're going to hit a road bump, and you're going to procrastinate until you can sigh and call in a favor from a friend. That doesn't mean that you've made a mistake in challenging yourself. It means that you didn't notice that you assigned yourself to a high-risk category, and that in a normal world that's where failure piles up.

When I come into contact with my inborn will, it becomes clear that my problem isn't a weakness in motivation. I'm procrastinating because I'm *scared*. I think that I've bitten off more than I can chew and I'll fail. I recognize that most of the time that's a false narrative. I actually *can* do it.

When I was in fifth or sixth grade I noticed that I had a habit of putting off my homework as an undesirable thing, every day, but that when finally at night I picked up the math worksheet and started finding the answers, I really liked it. The next day I did the same thing. I avoided my homework out of fear of drudgery for as long as I could, and then five minutes into it found myself having a right good time. Haven't I done something like that all my life?

We actually make a lot of good choices, every day, and yet we berate ourselves out of all proportion when it looks like some project or relationship is going south. What if I took another look and found that my issue isn't procrastination. It's that obstacles show up. They don't show up because there's something wrong with me. They just show up. Maybe the obstacles are an interesting part of the puzzle. Maybe if I'm delaying completion of something, then there's an interesting obstacle in my way. If I know that I'm steadfast by nature, the clutter of possible punishment for failure disappears. I can fail on my own terms, which comes to about twenty percent of the time if I'm normal. Or I can find my way around the interesting obstacle and complete the task.

In the end, will is all about how mature you feel. To give up a task prematurely requires you to belittle yourself, and claim a kind of childishness. You probably call it being irresponsible. You might remember the early days of grammar school, when you learned the plan of the adults was to turn you into one of them. They operated in a world of rules and jobs and calendars and responsibilities. It made you shudder. From the six-year-old's vantage, the adult world is beyond confusing. When you call yourself lazy, you're reverting to that six-year-old. Basically, you want to go hide out in an easier, less-demanding world, the play-world of kids. It's a sensible plan. We all choose it at times, and there's no reason to get down on yourself for it. But then the pesky task you've avoided rears up on the calendar again, and what do you do? The divine form of will doesn't swoop in and complete your tasks. It does something far simpler. It reminds you that you've done pretty well up to now and that by and large you've been an adult most of your adult life. It reminds you that your spine is already straight, and as soon as you notice that, you sit up straighter. It reminds you that no one expects you to get everything done overnight and that plodding along is the name of the game. And you start plodding along again. A nice part of divine will is that it isn't grim. *Acting* like an adult can be grim. You've probably had a boss or two who wanted you to think that nothing on earth was more important than your latest work project. Divine will doesn't yell at you or berate you for missing a deadline. That's fake will. Divine will is mature, yes, but it's also cheery and forgiving. Divine will reminds *me*, for instance, that my chair is comfortable, my computer is working, the heat is on, and I can write these paragraphs now, on deadline, and that's my whole job. Sure, it might be a slog sometimes, but so what? It's not my job to beat myself up, and my job isn't my life. And, oh yeah, I get just about everything done.

Feeling mature is no different from *being* mature. Having a presence around or in me – a divine body-form – that expresses maturity as a thought and a sensation and an energetic feeling is the same thing as being mature. My inner support is made obvious, and it takes care of my finishing these paragraphs. If I'm stuck and find myself avoiding a task, I can look inside *me* and find my personal and divine will. It's there for me in a pinch. Body-forms are always reminders of my own, ever-present inner support. If I call myself lazy, then I've forgotten that I'm carrying will around with me all the time.

Like the other divine body-forms, will is simple and plain. While the body-forms have a kind of beauty when seen inside, recognizing them is not an entryway into a spiritual bliss state. They are functional, and they help us perform as human beings in the complicated real world around us. They're more like a helpful partner's pat on the back than a trained guide's map or the captain of a ship's orders. Like the other body-forms, divine will nudges you that your problem – whether it's a momentary procrastination or a lifetime believing that you're lazy – isn't quite what you think it is, and that you might already have the solution inside.

The Bridge

As with curiosity and strength, the concept of this divine body-form offers you a bridge to take you from your suffering in a particular way to relief from that suffering. You can move from your own feeling of immaturity or laziness to a more complete understanding of your own will that you carry with you, deep down inside. This can result in a movement from your feeling a lack of will – I want to be more steadfast in life – to an easier time of it when tackling complicated projects. This divine aspect of God is one way to get from here to there, but for it to catch hold and make itself fully known to you, it needs to be moved from your mind – the concept of divine will – to your body, where it can take form as if an organ inside you.

The Body-Form of Will

Like all the divine body-forms, *will* opens up inside your body, usually at the bottom of your stomach. After your regular organs gently move themselves out of the way, you'll see a mountain suddenly appear. Even though it fits inside your abdomen, it is as big as a real mountain. Craggy and solid, weighty and substantial, the mountain of *will* is usually white. You might experience it as the mountain one time, and then other times, on separate journeys into your inner self, an object will turn white or a white stripe will appear or the air inside you might be detailed with white flakes. All of these can represent pure will as you explore your divine self.

A separate but related body-form, called *universal will*, can also appear. This one represents not just your ability to get something done, but your overall sense of your own maturity and steadfastness. You can be in the middle of an inner journey with a space in your torso at your disposal, and a color or object manifesting, when you sit up straight and feel your spine turn into a platinum bar an inch wide and quarter inch thick, running from your tailbone all the way to your cranium. It feels like the platinum bar has actually lodged there. These body-form experiences have a feeling of reality even though they are disconnected from your cellular, physical self. For a few minutes at least, you become an embodied metaphor for the answer to the issue you've been facing.

As usual, the experience has taken you only one way on the bridge, from the concern over your self-proclaimed laziness or immaturity to the reservoir of steadfastness inside you. The body-form is the representation of that steadfastness. It isn't the steadfastness itself. But over the course of a number of visits, each time returning to your familiar self refreshed and energized with a feeling of maturity, you might just start to believe that the steadfastness you're seeing has a real source, and that source is inside you.

Maybe you're already a lot more mature than you thought, and maybe you're already steadfast.

Chapter 7

Compassion

O ur first year of marriage was pretty easygoing.
Annie and I met late in life, and each of us had
built up some skills in curing or bypassing a lot of
the usual conflicts. Put another way, life had
beaten us down enough that we knew not to provoke
another lashing. It's not that money and jealousy were no
longer treacherous, but a little eye-rolling behind the other
person's back was sufficient to get through the day. When
the pandemic showed up, we adjusted pretty quickly, and
blessed ourselves for having such routine, boring lives
already.

And then I made the mistake of going back to school.
It wasn't just the Sanskrit. The other classes, too, quickly
wore me down. The problem was that I didn't know how to
shut up, and all the classes were seminars. No lectures, just
open discussions where anyone – especially me – could
poke their nose in. Never invite a congenital know-it-all to
an open conversation.

After every class, I turned off the Zoom feed and limped from my office to the living room, where Annie would look up cheerfully and ask, "Talk too much?"

Sometimes I muttered back, "I hate myself." Or I just stared at my kind wife, slack-jawed, while my mind played back the Grateful Dead lyric, "Please don't dominate the rap, jack, when you got nothing new to say." Over and over.

I tried the usual cures: Pre-class admonitions to speak no more than four times. File cards on which I ticked off each time I spoke – nine was the fewest, more than two times my self-imposed quota. Under-the-breath self-thrashings. I started waking up in the middle of the night, upset at myself. Finally I asked Annie for help. Her response: "Tell me more."

She didn't offer a cure, or an explanation. She left all that to me. She did ask me questions, and encouraged me to talk about it. Slowly, I started to uncover – again – both the genesis of my narcissism, which has something to do with being brought up in a know-it-all household, and the triggering aspects of being back in school, where I'm to be judged and graded on my intelligence. Ugh, I disliked thinking about this even more than I dislike beets. But Annie didn't let go. "Tell me more," she said, day after day.

And eventually, simply by revealing my suffering to Annie and therefore to myself, I didn't hate myself like I was the pariah student. I moderately disliked myself like I was beets. That was enough. I could even feel sorry for myself. And while my logorrhea continued, to be fixed the following semester perhaps, my self-loathing released itself into the ether.

What Annie showed me, and what with her tutelage I started to feel for myself, is the aspect of God known as "compassion."

Pure Compassion as a Concept

Compassion is the love that arises in the presence of suffering.

Let's break that sentence down. "Compassion" is a word that we use liberally, across lots of different kinds of circumstances, to describe a feeling. When the word "compassion" shows up, it comes with a sense of richness, fluidity, and fullness in the chest. You may notice some energy rising from chest to head. We believe that the word represents something that we offer to others, or to ourselves. But is that accurate? Not if I study the definition I've proposed closely.

Compassion *is the love that* arises in the presence of suffering. Compassion isn't the only kind of love; it's a form that love takes. We know of other forms of love – for instance silly love, passionate love, or sweet love. There's something specific about compassion's form of love. How can I discriminate it from other kinds of love?

Compassion is the love that *arises* in the presence of suffering. Compassion isn't manufactured. It arises, all on its own. I'm not compassionate, in the sense that it isn't something I do. It's more like a place where I find myself living. I find myself in the presence of compassion.

Compassion is the love that arises *in the presence of suffering*. Now we're getting down to brass tacks. For compassion to arise, suffering has to show up first. Suffering can be great: the grief that accompanies a loved one's death, or the difficulty of living in a bad marriage. Suffering can be trivial: a friend's slight, a broken martini glass. Either way, compassion arises, which means that it makes itself available.

The thing is, most of human interaction and much of the rest of life revolve around suffering. If you look for it,

compassion is always here, or just around the corner.
Think about suffering in all its manifestations.

- ❧ Most conversation is complaining about things that have gone wrong or are about to go wrong

- ❧ All news shows focus primarily on things going wrong; even the "good news" segments are about people helping people who are suffering

- ❧ Gossip generally homes in on the misfortune of others

- ❧ Most entertainment focuses on suffering. Sitcoms revolve around conflict, novels torture their characters with a new conflict every page or two, love songs typically depict yearning and lost-love suffering

- ❧ Most joking around is irony that focuses on the absurdity of the difficulty of life

- ❧ Most of my interior dialogue is presenting the danger of missed opportunities, past or future

- ❧ Most families when forced close together by circumstances digress into petty conflicts and grievances

- ❧ Catharsis and good feelings last a very short time compared with their lead-up of suffering

It all sounds pretty grim, right? I'm sure you want to argue with this litany, and you probably have a point. I'm leaving out lots of time spent in daydreaming and happy work and good times with friends and family. My guess is that 80 percent of human interaction is related to suffering. Your guess may be that it's 40 percent or less. Either way, there's plenty of opportunity, daily if not hourly, for compassion to arise in the presence of suffering.

Most of us confuse sympathy for compassion. The usual mental response to a close friend's complaint is, "Yes, I know that one. I can help you through it." The problem with sympathy is twofold. First, it takes the suffering out of the victim's experience of it and places it in some paradigm that you, the so-called helper, have developed for yourself. Instead of it being about the friend, it's really about you. Second, by saying, "Yes, I know that one," you have forestalled any further exploration by the suffering friend. You've stopped him or her at their first identification, which might be accurate or might not. It's actually worse than helpful to say, "Yes, I've suffered in the same way." I know, I know. This is counterintuitive. But let's see what happens if you don't use those words, and don't try to help.

What happens if you say to your friend, "Oh, you're suffering. Tell me more."?

In my experience, the friend vents and vents and vents for as long as it takes. And once the venting is over, a different emotion than the pain of suffering overtakes the friend. Sometimes it's an understanding that more was going on than he or she first noticed. Sometimes it's a feeling of relief, as if the suffering has let go a bit. Sometimes it's a feeling of embarrassment, as if noticing that the suffering was exaggerated. Whatever the change, it provides the friend with some distance from the emotional grip that created the complaint in the first place.

When we're complaining, we're defending ourselves against an enemy, an attack, or an unwanted feeling. When we're done defending, we get quiet and let what's here show up. What's here, inevitably, is compassion. The only thing in the way of love – which is the natural state of things

in relationship – is our defenses. The easiest way to drop
our defenses is to release them full force into the world and
watch them burn themselves out temporarily. That's why
we vent. That's why we complain. Usually we cut off our
complaining before the defense is exhausted, though, and
move onto something else before taking advantage of the
respite of compassion.

The Bridge

Knowing compassion conceptually offers its bridge to
take you from your suffering to relief from that suffering.
You can move from your own sense of suffering, from grief
or loss or self-loathing, to a more complete understanding
of your own compassion for the child or adult inside who is
hurting. By entering into the story of your own brand of
suffering, you can find the part of you inside that is built to
love you past any suffering. This divine aspect of God is one
way to get from here to there, but for it to catch hold and
make itself fully known to you, it needs to be moved from
your mind to your body.

The Body-Form of Compassion

Here's what *compassion* is like in the torso, when
noticed as a body-form: You can find it anywhere, but it
resides most often in the chest. The torso contains a
metaphoric heart that is roughly brick shaped and spans
the interior of the sternum. This subtle heart has a
pericardium, a thin layer of penetrable skin, just like your
real heart. Inside it's usually liquid, although I've also
experienced it as feathers. But you might just as well find
compassion in your belly or head, in a cloudy or solid form,
a small streak or speckles, or a big swath or filling
everything. It's emerald green, and occasionally appears as

an emerald. It feels rich and spreads easily, warming the interior.

When true *compassion* arises, you don't need to do anything. If it arises with a friend, you'll find yourself smiling and asking the friend to keep describing their suffering. If you're feeling compassion for yourself, you'll notice that it's easier to live with your past shames, guilts, and embarrassments. Their emotive force seems to dissolve in its presence. You're not just self-forgiving. You feel love and, well, compassion, for the person who lived through those things and did those things. You're your own confessional priest, and your own protector and savior. The main thing is, *compassion* doesn't usually have to *do* anything. It's enough to be present with the suffering, and given enough time and attention, it will move away and allow lightness to return.

Compassion is light, hearty, and positive.

Chapter 8

Power

S ome years ago one of my kids was having a hard time at school in Colorado. I had experienced marginal semesters in college, so I delayed action for a while. But now it was time.

Was he taking good care of himself? Was he protecting his permanent record? Was he listening to the good advice that was coming from his parents? I prepared myself to have a talk with him. But just before I picked up the phone, I stopped.

Something felt weird, like I was missing a variable, an essential component that I needed before I could effectively get all my well-thought-out points across. Why did I hesitate? Wasn't the role of parent important? As my mind drifted, the lightbulb went off. I'm being a doctor, not a parent, I thought. I've diagnosed what malady the kid has, and now I'm going to get him the treatment. But he's twenty years old. Why am I treating him like he's six? If I'm still in that old father-doctor role, am I also sticking to the old diagnosis? And should I be the doctor anymore?

Now I was ready to dial the phone. When Andrew answered, I said only, "Hey, I'm free this coming weekend. Would you mind having a visitor?" Fortunately, he was happy to receive me. I bought a ticket and Friday found myself on the tarmac strolling into the Durango, Colorado, terminal where Andrew was waiting. I thought to myself, "I don't know him. I don't know Andrew." It became a mantra. I kept it going in my mind as we drove into Durango, checked into my hotel room, and walked over to Main Street together. We chit-chatted, but nothing important. I kept the mantra going. "I don't know him. I don't know Andrew." I was blocking out all my preconceptions about Andrew with three words: I don't know.

As we strolled Main Street with its tourist stores and restaurants, I found myself getting annoyed at Andrew opening his flip phone and apologizing as he stopped and talked. It happened every 200 feet, at least once a block. Then I asked myself whether I needed to be annoyed. "I don't know," I reminded myself. "I don't know Andrew." Calmer now, I started listening in to his brief conversations. After four blocks, tears came to my eyes.

Andrew was the friend who everyone else depends on for advice. He was answering questions about work, romance, what was happening in town, about feeling bad, about the daily difficulties of life. He was that guy. I had never known that Andrew was that guy. I would never have known without stopping my diagnoses and replacing them with "I don't know." My tears were tears of gratitude.

Pure Power as a Concept

Most of us think of power as some form of control. Powerful people control weak people. Powerful ideas shut out weak ideas. Powerful emotions overcome weak emotions. So we think that power is opposed to weakness. But don't we also believe that strength is opposed to weakness? What distinguishes weakness of control from other weaknesses?

Controlling things requires mental energy. Unlike the simple capacity to do something, which we call *strength*, or the steadfastness to complete things, which we call *will*, our idea of *power* is that it requires constant, obsessive energy. The king is ever-vigilant, or dethroned.

The false form of *power* is compulsive behavior. Energy is continually expended to first rise to the top and then extend that status quo as long as possible. Politicians repeat their narrow view of possibilities over and over until others believe that theirs is the only choice. Abusive spouses erupt repeatedly to keep their partner in line. People with OCD try to use a form of magic to keep the routine from being changed. Underlying the false form of power is a hidden self-hatred that rests in a belief that without power, the person would not be loved or found worthy. Many CEOs are among the most damaged and insecure people in the world, as are many actors, generals, and politicians. Their narcissistic need for control provides them with the energy to compulsively rise to the top, taking no prisoners along the way. Not all CEOs, actors, generals, and politicians are helplessly narcissistic. But those are the kinds of positions where narcissists aim their lives, so they fill those positions in society disproportionately.

The true form of *power* is quite different. Instead of the compulsive energy being directed toward outward achievement and control of others, a like amount of energy is directed inward toward self-discovery. The kind of work that is involved in body-form experiences leads toward this kind of power.

Power is a kind of activating force that results in self-discovery. This is your own drive to question cultural assumptions and explore who you are without them. When you've made a number of excursions into your beliefs, power starts to emerge. It doesn't appear in the way you might expect. It isn't a dynamo or a lightning bolt or hammer.

It's stillness.

A bad boss thinks they know better, and tells you what to do. A good boss thinks you are the expert and asks lots of questions. The good boss is starting from the stillness and emptiness of "I don't know." In this way, power is the peaceful, empty stopping-off place that precedes dialogue or action.

What's left when your rote beliefs are sidelined is a sense of peace, accompanied by a kind of silence and stillness that might precede any activity. "I don't know" precedes divine *curiosity*. There's *power* in the absence of preconception, and it's peaceful and still.

The Bridge

Knowing about power conceptually is the bridge you might need to reduce that nagging feeling that you need to be prepared all the time, and allow yourself to trust the moment and your own spontaneous, intuitive intelligence. Maybe aggression and dominance aren't what's called for this time. Maybe the silence of I don't know can be preparation enough.

The Body-Form of Power

Many of my clients at some point experience a black, still space that starts in their torso and either spreads through their body or, more commonly, leads out beyond the boundaries of the skin. This body-form of power at first seems empty, but it's not a deficient emptiness. The black stillness that extends spatially in any direction has a richness to it, as if the emptiness was made of something indescribable. The blackness can expand out into a whole new dimension, or it can gain galaxies, or it can annihilate everything in its path. It doesn't have to do those things, and each of those is a new exploration of a related, but different experience. The body-form of power is simple, empty of objects, and still and peaceful.

The power that it restores in you is humble, patient, non-compulsive, and uninterested in control. Like other body-forms, it encourages a concern for accuracy, for objectivity and for not holding onto common preconceptions. It gives you an appreciation for doubt as a tool for exploration, and a distrust of certainty. It's energetic, so complacency doesn't factor in. Power respects the still point from which anything new can emerge.

Power is simple, calm, and directed.

So those are the *lataif,* the big five aspects of God that can build a complete person. Before we go on to some other body-forms inside you, let's find out a little more about their recent discovery.

Shapes of Truth

Chapter 9

Credit

Hameed Ali is a Kuwaiti-born American spiritual leader who moves through a room full of students head down, with little notice and no pomp. His speech is unaffected and full of good humor. His shoulders are squared and at ease, and he is difficult if not impossible to affront. Now in his 70s, Hameed Ali's round face is usually cast with thoughtfulness, and when he raises his head from musing, his eyes glint with inquiry. He often punctuates a serious statement with a soft grin, and serious conversations with him often gravitate to the topic of love. He can be very funny.

Under the pen name A.H. Almaas, Ali writes prolifically. A few titles: *The Void, Faces of Unity, The Pearl Beyond Price - Integration of Personality into Being: An Object Relations Approach, The Point of Existence - Transformations of Narcissism in Self-Realization, Diamond Heart* Books 1-6.

He is on the short list of contemporary spiritual masters. Ali oversees a curriculum of his own making, a school that I have attended, a seminary for training teachers, and about 5,000 current students who pass through his process in groups of thirty to 200 that form regularly in the United States and Europe. Many more thousands of people have read his books. He is scandal free, has no penchant for chasing the skirts or trousers of his students, drives a Tesla, and I'm told he is the kind of host you find wearing an apron as he cleans the dishes after dinner.

The thinker he's compared to most often is Ken Wilber, who like Ali and unlike most contemporary spiritual masters is interested in bringing a straightforward scientific method to what has traditionally been called metaphysics. But for Ali, science is an attitude more than a tool. It's quite popular nowadays to show that quantum mechanics or neurology or energy field study proves that a state of being found in Hinduism or Buddhism or another *ism* is true. That's not Ali. He started out as a physical scientist – he was a PhD candidate at the University of California at Berkeley physics lab – but he purposely gave all that up to pursue first psychology and then metaphysics.

Psychological and metaphysical truths just seemed more compelling to him than physics. He was drawn to them as the next step in a life of curiosity and truth-seeking. They became his purpose, too.

Ali is known as the depth psychology guy, and his course of study fits well within the modern, New Age cadre of spiritual masters. These self-realization gurus often blend a modern understanding of psychodynamics with ancient wisdom to provide an efficient path to enlightenment. The problem of the ego has always been around. Buddhism, Hinduism, and Christianity all wrestle with the influence of the ego, how it tricks us into narrow conflicts and beliefs, and keeps our eyes on surface desires while blocking our view of everyday life's inherent beauty, wisdom, love, and truth. To Buddhists, the goal might be to get rid of the ego. In Hinduism, it's moving away from a small self with little or no awareness of God and into a big Self as a God-soaked being. In Christianity the ego problem is summed up as getting the plank out of your eye; your own false beliefs are like cataracts blocking the true light of the world. Along all these paths, the ego is considered a distortion machine that needs to be cleaned up or done away with in order to reach a higher state or states. But lacking a framework for how the ego develops and functions as a process, the ancient traditions tended to be scattershot in their methods to get it out of the way. Some recommend repetitive exercises of chanting, or meditation, or breathwork, or physical concentration that result in either a gradual or sudden release from the ego's tentacles. Others say, "Just do it." Techniques are applied, and if nothing much happens for the student, and the ego stubbornly holds on, the answer is often to apply more rigor – like bodybuilders with their weights graduating into more repetitions.

Other New Age leaders had noticed that the language of Freud – the unconscious, the ego, the superego and id, avoidance and denial, neurosis and psychosis – could be useful for students trying to manage their ego disturbances. Ali noticed something beyond that. He saw that the student could use the same concepts to help go beyond managing their ego, and actually shed it. The point wasn't to get a better ego. By understanding the ego's mechanics, the student could move outside the ego, into a land of great freedom.

Ali developed a detailed process for students to move backward through their built-up ego defenses, removing them one after another. Each time an ego defense fell, a little bit of paradise arrived, often opening up divine body-forms and other spiritual states and realms.

Ali named the process he discovered the Diamond Approach or Diamond Heart, and the institution he developed to teach the process the Ridhwan School. (Ridhwan is a Sufi term that means something like equanimity.) He and his trained teachers take students on a step-by-step path of removing ego obstacles and watching a bigger reality flood in.

Most spiritual masters settle for one discovery and one radically new teaching. But it turns out that Ali isn't just the depth psychology guy. He's also the essential aspects guy, the person who discovered the thirty-five divine body-forms that this book describes. The catalog at the end of the book is largely his. All I have done in the book is put them in a context that is understandable in a particular way. Ali applies them in a different context – his school.

Ali spends part of most days shut up in an office with a single platonic partner – Karen Johnson. (They were a trio for several years before their third, Faisal Muqaddam, went off to teach on his own.) They don't spend a lot of time asking how or why. They stay with the *what*. What's here? What does it look like? What is it doing? The idea is that eventually everything has a chance to emerge. Their one rule is to stay present in seeking the truth of what is going on right now. Ali's discoveries, lectures, and books come out of these one-on-one continuing explorations of reality, as well as resulting talks to groups of students. I studied under Ali and other Diamond Approach teachers for ten years.

I believe that Ali's discovery is monumental. When he turned away from physics, he didn't set out to explore a wilderness or mountain, the skies above, or the hidden realities of the outside world. He set out to explore his own, *inner* self. At some point, he noticed himself taken over by something called presence, which was followed by a feeling of being part of an essence. When his self-inquiry focused on essence, the parts of essence – the divine body-forms, which he named "essential aspects" – simply showed up. He didn't expect them, and he didn't arrive at them through applied logic. They appeared, all on their own, as a byproduct of his investigations.

Ali's attitude of "What's here without preconception?" is more difficult to attain than most people, even most scientists, might think. The usual scientific method includes a step called "setting an hypothesis." If prejudice and expectation are thoroughly removed, hypotheses disappear. Maybe that's what Hameed had over other psychological-spiritual explorers heading into the same explorations. Maybe he was simply more ready to let what would appear, appear.

Look into your body.

See what arises.

Explore it.

Shapes of Truth

Chapter 10

≈୬୬≈

A Little Plato

S canning philosophy, religion, and metaphysics
through the ages, it's hard to find anything that
directly connects to Ali's discovery. The thirty-five
divine body-forms just aren't replicated anywhere.
Only the Sufi – who discovered five, six, or seven of them,
depending on which text you believe – seem to be at all
aware of them. Those are the *lataif* that Ali identified
toward the beginning of his discovery of the bigger realm
that encompassed them. In close study, the structures and
purposes of the thirty-five divine body-forms don't
conform to the obvious potential cognates: They're not
organized into the tree of life of Kabbalah. They're not a
path like the uncoiling chakras, and the body-form colors
don't correspond to the relatively recent formulation of
chakra colors. No system of somatic psychology presents
them. No famous philosophers through the ages have

presented them. They're not characterized in the realms described in ancient Buddhist or Hindu texts.

And yet they seem to be a fundamental underpinning of understanding that might associate with *any* philosophy or religion. They are more building blocks than path. With that in mind, the one tantalizing possibility of a precursor who knew about them is Socrates. The divine body-forms seem to correspond to the idea of a category of concepts and a way of understanding known to the Greek philosopher, as described by his chronicler, Plato.

In Plato's *Republic*, Socrates describes a hierarchy of things and ideas. At the highest state are found the Platonic ideals – the perfect, distinct presence of nouns of value. Slightly below the Platonic ideals can be found the mathematical concepts. Together, the Platonic ideals and mathematics share a space of perfection and undistorted intelligence. The lower two states below them are those of common-sense reality, including concrete nouns or sensible objects like chairs and trees, and, at the bottom, perceptions and unexamined opinions like "the earth is flat." In short, the hierarchy from top to bottom traces meaning from divine wisdom to rank idiocy.

The highest realm of pure Platonic forms is filled only with *abstract* nouns of value. "Chairness" isn't elevated to this realm. "Love" belongs there, and "grace" and "strength." But chairness simply describes an idealization of a concrete object. It doesn't grant value, and has no association with good or bad. A concrete noun has no opposite; non-chairness is an absurdity that contains everything in the world that isn't the idealized chair. "Weakness," however, is a distinct thing in and of itself, just as "strength" is.

So one characteristic of the abstract nouns of value, and in turn the thirty-five divine body-forms that we've been discussing, is that each is unique and distinguishable from every other one. Another characteristic is that each implies an opposite that also is unique and distinguishable. (Which is not to say that the negative opposites share space in the highest realm; they don't seem to.)

Those are the kinds of conditions that would allow for a system of symbols – like the body-forms we are exploring – that are unique, that are as universally known as the utility of each word that they represent, and that are comprehensible through comparison and association.

But we already have words. The word "virtue" is universal enough. Why would we need these body objects? What oomph might they give us?

Plato's *Meno* is a typical Socratic dialogue. It begins with Meno asking, "Can you tell me, Socrates – is virtue something that can be taught?"

Socrates responds that he can't answer Meno because he isn't sure what the word "virtue" means. The two men travel down Socrates' familiar path of defining terms. They spend most of the dialogue disagreeing on a definition for "virtue." They never arrive at a conclusive, common meaning. That doesn't mean Socrates and his pals fail. A lot happens along the way. What is left unsaid at the end of the dialogue is that questioning assumptions – defining terms – may temporarily delay a solution to the original question, but enters a new, fascinating, unprejudiced world that unfolds and blossoms in real time. Defining terms, questioning assumptions, opening your ears – all of these describe a process that rejects pat beliefs and knowledge and lets you start over without preconceptions. Social, communal reality has a way of narrowing and changing the meanings of words so that they'll serve some productive function. "Virtue" becomes "patriotism," if the state gets its way. "Generosity" becomes "charity," if the wealthy get their way.

By forcing myself to question assumptions – define terms – I've stopped myself in a territory that only asks "what" something is, and doesn't care a whit for why it's there or where it's going. Or even what it might interact with. Defining a term interrupts my mind's tendency to careen through a tangle of associations and memories and prior beliefs. What is virtue? Right now. What is it? What does it mean right now? Can you describe it? Does it have characteristics? Independent of circumstances, independent of its surroundings, what might it be?

This is exactly how the body-forms are experienced. If you ask your torso how they got there or why they're there, they will disappear. But if you just examine them, as is, when they appear in your body, you will eventually be rewarded. The reward is a visit to your own acre of contentment.

As Ali repeatedly offers his Ridhwan students, all you ever need to do is attune to the truth of what is here, now. If in doubt, look at what's happening now. At the "what" of the now. The implication is that doing that alone will eventually bring a person to the source, which in spiritual matters is the divine.

Body-forms don't feel like meaningful thoughts. Nor do they feel like metaphors. As experienced, they stand out as singular within themselves, not needing explanation or analysis. The feeling is akin to jumping into a pool, or being surrounded by nature. These body-forms are like the redwood trees I pass on my daily run, standing out elegantly from the indeterminate tangle of the forest as if they weren't sprouted but carved by a divine hand.

My regular old mind generates *ideas* about these experiences, and the ideas can assemble themselves into a belief system, or a cosmology, or some other abstract structure. But coming into the body-form experience itself has no need to be elaborated like that. Its power is in the moment of the experience itself. Everyday meaning – thoughts about consequences – feels like a shadow in comparison with the vivid reality that shows up as the body-form's wisdom.

Broadly speaking, our familiar words get contaminated with ego impressions, socially derived belief systems, and the stories that build up our personalities. The mind isn't a very trustworthy place. It tends to fixate and distort as it draws on its own fallible memory – the past – to try to create a plausible story for the future. It confuses what it knows – the original shared meaning of the word – with what it believes through a biased, personal experience. I'm talking psychology here, not physics. Math and measurement have a factual perfection that the mind can grasp and stay tuned to. Human behavior isn't measured like that. Preferences and decisions are fallible. The abstract nouns of value are oriented to us as humans trying to operate in the world, and in their usual form they change as society changes.

The body, meanwhile, is an undistorted machine. It doesn't have an unconscious self and conscious self that are in conflict and trying their damnedest to align. The body is less complicated. The body knows how to develop, which it does a lot of during its first twelve or so years, and how to keep vigilant and maintain itself, which is mostly what it does the rest of our lives. When we're adults, the body is primarily in maintenance mode, until it has run its course. Each of any individual's 37 trillion or so cells has a monitoring device; when its alarm rings, the cell sends out a call for the medics, and repair troops come streaming to the rescue. The body is an expert truth machine.

1. Check what is going on.
2. Search for error (lack of wholeness).
3. Repair when necessary.

That's just about all that the body does. As a basically truthful entity, the body is a more logical repository than the mind when the soul wants to explore its values without distortion. What would you be left with if an idea was cleansed of distortion and seen for what it really is? It might be more like a feeling than a conceptual idea, more of an experience than a thought. *Strength* might feel full-blooded. *Trust* might look like a white light. *Power* might feel like a shining, peaceful blackness. These are ideal states of being, and yet they can be known and appreciated as our own. That's wild.

What if I was perfect? What if scenes of awe spilled out right in front of me? Would I ever be the same? Would my life take on new colors?

Chapter 11

Love Is Not An Emotion

I'm all in favor of a hidden universe that encompasses concepts like God, eternal truths, immortal souls, and my fervent hope that my worst acquaintances will shape up before they die. But I'm also reliant on rationality, which includes the problem of objectivity in a flawed world, and figuring things out for myself, with my brain. So when I took up dating again, as a middle-aged, divorced man, I created a couple of spreadsheets.

Anyone who's dated later in life knows how grisly it can be. For one thing, my gender – especially that portion that is heterosexual – leaves a lot to be desired. We're a bad-tempered bunch. But while the other gender is better socialized, any individual member might be annoying. Not you, of course. I'm talking about those other women. Since online dating is a bit of a numbers game, my spreadsheets were designed to narrow the field to "likelies," while also giving me an out – look, there's another fish in the sea, and she's right there in row four – when things didn't go so well. By keeping my eye on the prize, I might not have to address my latent misogyny in the face of a woman not particularly liking my habits or my face.

One of the spreadsheets was a series of checkboxes to keep score. My friend Kevin who has a PhD in economics from NYU designed it for me. Its rows were the names of women whose online profiles interested me. The columns were labeled CONTACT, AGREEMENT TO MEET, FIRST DATE, SECOND DATE, THIRD DATE. The next column, if I had bothered with it, might have been GOING STEADY.

The second spreadsheet, which was linked through a pivot table, was filled out after the first date, and updated after the second and third. It was a doublecheck to see whether the qualities I wanted in a partner were being met. I had four non-negotiables, and a fifth category called the grab-bag, which listed about sixty qualities that were flexible so long as I didn't have to give up too many of them. These latter were behavioral patterns such as "doesn't leave dirty dishes out," "wakes up early," "prefers bluegrass to country." The Big Four non-negotiables were "Get Each Other's Jokes," "Has a Spiritual Path," "Sexually Compatible" (duh), and "Kind." This was pre-Trump, so I wasn't picky about political party; at the time the wrong politics was a fault that could be overlooked, more a grab bag quality.

If I could check off all five boxes, and she was willing, I was prepared to be hijacked by Cupid and head into the sweet and then terrible thing called falling in love. My spreadsheets would guide me to the perfect partner. She would have all Four and would meet me more than halfway on the grab bag.

My five categories could have been labeled "needs." We learn about romantic love through movies, novels, and stories that follow the consistent pattern: Boy and girl (or same-sex lovers) meet, find common ground and fall in love, and then one betrays the other by not satisfying a need (usually commitment), and when the miscreant realizes his or her mistake and comes crawling back with a willingness to fulfill that missing need, the wayward mate is accepted. The kiss appears on the screen and the credits roll. From Jane Austen to Judd Apatow, it's always the same. The general idea is that we look for someone who meets our needs in a compatible way and doesn't demand too much from their needs in return. Finding Mr. or Ms. or Mx. Right is somewhat transactional – my needs are filled in turn for my filling your needs. To the extent that the equation can be held up over time, the partnership is more or less successful. I'm not saying this is how it should be, just that our culture tells us to think about love this way. In the cultural literature, what is known as unconditional love is reserved for the relationship of parents to children, and is usually described in a mythical or mysterious tone.

Since most of life is transactional – we work for money, which we then trade for food and shelter; we *exchange* presents and well wishes; we *sacrifice* for our children and *spend* time with friends – it makes perfect sense that love would be its own *quid pro quo*. And as long as I lived that, I got nowhere in dating. Don't get me wrong. I met some fascinating people and enjoyed some lovely and loving relationships over the ten years that I was off-and-on in the dating market. I learned a lot about myself, and felt that I was becoming a better person.

But when I hit the love jackpot in 2016, it wasn't because Annie met my spreadsheet criteria (although, of course, she did.) And by the way, just so you aren't totally creeped out by my callous spreadsheets, I had abandoned them long before I met Annie. It's not that I didn't need them; they had just become fully internalized.

But instead of looking for each other's use value, from our very first date Annie and I more or less ignored the notion of exchanging needs. Instead we made ourselves vulnerable to each other. We talked about what we were ashamed of in ourselves. We talked about our most terrible selves and our most deficient selves. We weren't stupid; we also showed off a lot. But eventually, we would come around to the self who spends all its time worried about what people think, and we exposed it. And you know what? Love showed up as a field that required no exchanges, no gifts, no promises, and few expectations. We were both surprised and relieved to be objects of fascination with little judgment.

What if that's what love is?

What if love is what shows up mechanically, in its most appropriate form, when two people meet without filtering each other through their defense systems? What if love is just what's there when you remove the fear? It doesn't mean you'll love everybody in the same way. There are different forms that love can take. But love has nothing to do with your needs or your defenses. It isn't something you're missing and need to get filled up. It is already there, always available beyond your defenses. This is decidedly not the rom-com or Shakespearean tragedy view.

Love is mostly fascination with the other. An easy portal into love is to grab someone and lock eyes with them. In a matter of seconds, all distance between the two of you disappears. That's it. That's love. There's nothing except the moment of the locked eyes, and the body fills with a sense of richness, absorption, and the vague notion that you're seeing into the soul of the other being. All you are doing is meeting someone without prejudice or fear.

But you need to make yourself vulnerable for it to happen. Eventually that very vulnerability stops being felt as a weakness – I'm exposed and that's dangerous – and transforms into a superpower. For Annie and me, our spontaneous vulnerability toward each other cut through a lot of crap – secrets, shames, and decrepit stories – that might have taken years to let unfold safely in the normal way. And in that lost time, we might have given up on each other in frustration.

So what does this field of love look like in the context of the body-forms? It has several manifestations. You've met one of them. *Compassion* is the love that rises in the presence of suffering. It's a particular form of love. You don't get to pick compassion, by the way. It is chosen for you when you find yourself talking to someone who is suffering. If you are not scared of their suffering and are vulnerable to exactly what they're saying and suggesting, you're stuck with compassion. You lose a sense of distance from the other person, a sense of needing to do anything, and you feel a green sensation inside while engaged with fascination in the complaint of your friend. All the forms of love are like that. They have their own appropriateness, which is a good thing. Most of you wouldn't want passionate love to show up when you were talking to the Trader Joe's clerk in a field of universal love.

Pink Fluffy Love

Personal love – which is your default – is named here for its literal appearance. Pink fluffy love is a little girl in a frock in a field of daisies. It's a little boy rolling down a grassy hill. It's ebullient, goofy, wide-eyed, and pleased with itself and with everything around it. It's cotton candy in a cool breeze, and a pink sunset on a warm day. And it's you, as a mature adult, if you let yourself see who you are when nothing is required of you. It's as if your inner child is enchanted by everything beautiful and new in its view. That's actually who you are when moving through the world, whether you're driving through your neighborhood, or daydreaming at work, or people-watching from a sidewalk café. Relax, look around, and you'll find yourself a silly goose. I know the adult world is supposed to be grim. Bad things will happen, and you certainly won't notice any pink fluffy love when they do. But when you get past the tough spots, it's all about play.

For many of us, it's embarrassing to discover that our default participation in love is silliness, or play. At the end of the book, I discuss the obstacles that get in the way of each of the divine body-forms. For now, it's enough to know that most people have an aversion to being seen as childlike. But this isn't an imitative childishness, like conversing in baby talk. It's just an appreciation that play and fascination are at the root of the human experience of the field of love.

For a child, play means pulling something close – a toy, a sprinkler, an E-Z Bake Oven, a sibling – and testing out its connections with other things. Pulling things close is Step One. Testing its connections – fitting things together – is Step Two. Satisfaction with the result – learning all the way to meaning – is Step Three.

Adult life is no different. The puzzles are different. We pull variables into our local proximity, manipulate them toward a particularly satisfying result, and when successful, announce that we're done, or that we've found the meaning. Whether we're solving a mathematical problem, looking over a profit and loss statement, or mowing the lawn, we're following the three steps in the same order and pattern as a three-year-old at play. A physicist, a corporate executive, and a gardener all default to pink, fluffy love when they examine their interest in securing their current place in the world.

This is also the love that you can feel for a complete stranger. It is simple delight. It can have the effect of forming a cosmic bubble that traps the two of you in a place of mutual good humor. Being delighted by the bank clerk in the field of personal love doesn't have anything to do with wanting to jump her bones or get her approval, or even getting your checking account balanced. You simply see her at her best, as a fellow human making her way through life. Instead of compassion, a stranger usually meets you with humor, which is a way of greeting each other with the recognition of the absurdity of the difficulty of life.

Merging Love

Personal love connects us to our love of ourselves and love of other people, animals, and things. Whether I'm experiencing myself or another, personal love is delighted in what it encounters.

Merging love takes that delight a step further. It represents the desire to softly melt into another and become one.

In the early months of life, a human baby has a sense of being within a dual unity, where mother and child are the same. To the infant, it's just a unity, unseparated at first from outside objects, but gradually in relationship to other things. The unity remains for a few months before the baby notices and becomes convinced that it is something different from its mother. Many mothers report the strange notion of being a single organism at first, believing that the baby's needs and feelings are signaled from within rather than communicated externally. To both mother and baby, the sensation is characteristically loving and nurturing, complete and fulfilling.

Maybe we retain something akin to a memory of that (though there's no sign that we have objective thinking that can be saved during the early months), but for whatever reason, as we mature we typically come to yearn for a feeling of dual unity, of being merged with another person. Instead of just being fascinated by the other person, we are unseparated, and feel the other person as if they are saturated through us, in us and of us. The afterglow of orgasm is a common experience of the feeling. More generally, merging love is the feeling of intimacy with a friend or lover, and the feeling of sharing with anyone.

Merging love as a body-form is a gold that is soft both in color and texture. If it isn't already melting when in the body, it is about to melt, like softened butter.

Melting into another may sound good, but it also has its dangers. What happens to me – my security in my sense of self – if my boundary is penetrated? What if the other person turns out to be too needy? What if I share too much, and I'm left wanting? What if the other turns out to be unworthy of my intimacy? And when we're cautious, and reserve merging love for an ideal potential mate, we run the risk of never experiencing it.

If it's not one thing, it's your mother. In this case, that old adage is true. Every chance to approach and sustain merging gold is likely to be corrupted by the original dual unity, either through proto-memory or through the cultural artifacts that bless that time as having been special. It's the only model we have for unconditional love, so it's no mystery that over time we believe that any other love is likely to be conditional. The corrupt belief is that our only chance for true intimacy is to return to that dual unity from infancy, either literally or by proxy. In some traditions, this yearning for absorption into mother is the ultimate test of the ego. The Bhagavad-Gita can be interpreted as the final battle to overcome the need for being merged with the mother.

Perversely, getting rid of the yearning or need to be merged with mother can open the possibility to merge with a person or divinity in your regular, adult life. Holding out an ideal always gets in the way of real life. We don't spend our lives in crystalline lakes, but in muddy puddles. Recognizing that this form of intimacy, merging gold, is always available to little old me, right now, opens my eyes to the possibility that it might not be dangerous to encounter it.

It's also helpful to note that the reward for moving through the yearning for a return to mother, and eventually abandoning it, is a door that opens for the soul to recognize and accept its capacity to merge with the divine. That kind of merging is associated with what New Agers call non-dualism.

Passionate Love

Depending on your taste for hedonism, the term "passionate love" might look forbidding or might cause you to drool. Or both. And you're partially right. Passion is passion, whether it's divine or miserably human. It feels like a driving force, an energy, almost instinctual in the way it reaches hungrily for pleasure.

Passionate love takes *merging love* and adds a portion of energetic desire. Rather than a yearning, it's a burning. As a body-form, it's got the taste and color of pomegranate, and the form of the fruit's nectar. It's highly energetic, buzzing with what Hindu sects call *shakti* or kundalini lifeforce. It represents the desire to be unseparated from a particular loved one, usually a romantic partner, but also from the divine as a personification. We might eventually merge with the loved one, but in the meantime we desire her or him.

Like the other forms of love, passionate love shows up when we're unguarded, available, and interested in the people and things around us. We don't choose what form love takes while we're in the unguarded attitude. We don't have to. Love is a field that is always there, but that is influenced by the relationships that emerge within it. Think of yourself and the object of your interest as locations that carry qualities of the divine. At any one time, your qualities may bubble up in a particular way that is detected by the field. The field conforms to what is bubbling through it, while maintaining its basic properties. Peculiarly, it decides for you what kind of love is present to be examined by you. You don't get to choose. But what you give up in free will, you gain back in the relief that true love – the love that arrives when you have removed or sidelined your defenses – is always appropriate to the situation.

Universal Love

You might have heard of cosmic consciousness or nondual ascension. *Universal Love* is noticed as both an entryway into cosmic consciousness and a landing in it, not as a place but more as an attitude. You like and love everything, from a single blade of grass to your partner to the most venal, brutal dictator. You can't help yourself. It's not that this is the best of all possible worlds. It's that everything in the world is, for the moment, as it is, and its wonders are all interconnected. Judgment is fully removed, and in its place, love is apparent as a permanent, sparkling field that extends through everything and beyond any known limits.

Obviously, it would be quite difficult to vote while engaged with cosmic consciousness. Except that you can love voting, too, and love both candidates, and love your free will and love your influence on the election. What you notice, too, is that the outcome is lovable no matter what it is. The conditions of cosmic consciousness don't favor free will, but they don't disallow anything, including free will, either.

Even if you can't imagine universal love without slipping into nihilism or blobbiness, you might be able to look at it as a nice place to visit.

That's it for the love facets of the divine. You might notice that they're all made of the same fabric, and they differ only in how close or separated you feel from your object of love. Personal love keeps the objects apart, but equally delightful and fascinating. It's playful. Merging love melts the two objects into each other. Passionate love pulls the two objects together where they can dance and move both independently and as one. Universal love draws all objects and the self together as a single, pervasive, unseparated unity of the many.

Shapes of Truth

Chapter 12

Guidance

B y my third child, I learned the appalling truth about teenagers: They lie. She stares you in the eyes and denies she smoked a cigarette, or tried weed, or skipped school, knowing that her pack of Marlboros and drug stash are still safely hidden behind the ceiling tile, and that you're not the type to check the car mileage for signs of vagabondage. She lies because she can, of course, but also because she has to. How else can she fully test her ability to thrive in the world by herself, unless she steps outside Dad's stupid, arbitrary boundaries?

I told my third and fourth child that the hardest job for a parent of teenagers is sorting the lies from the truth. My third child then took the route of never leaving any tracks, so I couldn't suspect her of anything. Smart kid. My fourth child, who by nature was not secretive, seldom lied. One day I asked him about that.

"Why don't you lie when I've caught you, like the other kids?" I asked.

"Because I don't get in trouble if I tell the truth," he said.

"You don't?"

"No, Dad, you only punish us for the lie, not for the deed."

Twenty years a parent, and I had never noticed that. Smarter kid.

Oddly, it makes sense. No broken rule is as damaging to my sense of humanity as is betrayal of trust. In the political realm, betrayal of trust always follows an act that is contrary to the rules. Standing up and declaring that you are going to break a rule is more acceptable than having people find out about it afterward and going through the motions of denial. Betrayal of trust means that the wrongdoer has adopted a view outside the norm or agreed-upon truth.

In English and many other languages, the words for "trust" and "truth" have identical roots. These words trace back to an early word for "tree." Solidity, uprightness, and unmistakability are all characteristics of trees, and qualities of trust and truth. Trust and truth may be complicated, but in the end they are always self-evident. I know truth when I see it, often as a feeling of landing in my body, and I know trust when I see it, often as a feeling of warmth and safety.

Like the big five – curiosity, strength, will, compassion and power – the body-forms for *trust* and *truth* are known to all my clients. Like the big five, they are experienced more often than most of the remaining body-forms.

Trust

Trust is the feeling that if I fall, someone or something will pick me up. When I trust someone, I believe that they will have my back. Friends are to be trusted. Charlton

Heston defined a best friend as the guy who will help you move the body without asking questions. Now that's trust! Trust feels supportive, and trust in other people means they will support me when I need them. It has an element of faith in it, no? Or something like faith, at least. "I trust you" means that I believe that you will respect my interests.

We live in a world of generalized distrust, where strangers live next door and tribal clans no longer exist outside remote areas such as the Amazon and New Guinea. We default to not trusting the politicians who are our chief social governors. Most of us have jobs where we can be fired without much cause, and so we distrust our bosses. If your partner keeps a lot of secrets, or cheats, you come to know that you can't trust them. Trust can be hard to come by in the civilized world. Who near me is telling the whole truth? Who near me has my back?

I might not even trust myself. When the chips are down will I wait to show my cards with confidence, or will I fold early? Do I support my endeavors with strength and steadfastness, or do I wimp out?

Inner work is difficult. It demands a willingness to torture myself by spending time reliving my suffering in order to discover its birthplace. What if instead of relief, I end up just feeling tortured, or re-traumatized, or belittled once again? What if I discover that I'm undeserving, or permanently damaged, or just plain childish? The leap of faith that inner work requires is the same thing as the trust we are talking about here, the embodied feeling that support accompanies me as I'm exploring my difficulties.

Often toward the beginning of an inner-body experience, a client may notice a shaft of white light with a yellow glow shining onto the first body-form, the one that represents my belief in my own suffering. That white-yellow light is like a pure sun, but it's inside me, not outside. It usually shows up early in the body-form encounter, and then disappears. It represents the trust that doing the inner work will be supported, even during the hard parts, and presumably will be rewarded somehow at the end. It is itself a reward of a kind; the feeling that I carry a divine form of trust within me is breathtaking, if you think about it. I don't need friends to be supported? I don't need a trustworthy boss or a non-secretive partner? I have the capacity for trust within me, at all times, ready to be tapped when I need it? Wow.

The worry, of course, is that I'll be taken advantage of. Untrustworthy people are usually not just unprincipled, but also selfish. If I'm worried about encountering one, the underlying belief is that that person will use me in a way that will be my loss and their gain. The rules are supposed to protect me from a human predator, but the untrustworthy one has broken the boundaries of the rules.

Interior trust, the body-form of white-yellow light, isn't a Pollyanna or Candide. It doesn't replace distrust of an untrustworthy person with naïve hope that they'll change. Instead, it faces the bad luck of being tricked or cheated as an anomaly that sticks out in a world that is rigged to the good. It doesn't let a life's typical series of unfortunate events – natural disasters, angry politics, unkind neighbors, conmen and grifters, embarrassing mistakes – leave you wanting. You have survived them and still can see that it's a universe and even a human race of support. If you're alive, you've been supported, by and large.

You won't find this white-yellow light element in the catalog of divine body-forms, for a technical reason. I've stuck with Hameed Ali's cosmology, which places this emanation of trust, which he calls Living Daylight, in a category of forms that are broader states of being. As this white-yellow light makes itself known later on his path, it becomes a pervasive guidance system of love that envelops everything inside and outside, and takes its place in Ali's catalog as one of four boundless dimensions.

But for the neophyte in the ways of the body-forms, it might as well be another body-form, helping you recognize the path to wisdom through exploration of suffering. It can simply be the sun burning through the morning fog and haze until it shines directly on your skin.

Truth

Truth is its own body-form. It is pure gold. It might be seen inside as solid or flowing or even a thin gold coating. It can be just the color gold, suffusing an otherwise empty space, or penetrating an object. It is shinier, bolder and richer than the gold of merging love. It seldom stands alone, but usually assists in the emergence of another body-form.

This is the truth found in the expression "The truth shall set you free." It serves to protect you, much as trust supports you, as you explore the false stories of the ego. The gold reminds you that you're safe when questioning long-held assumptions, or dismantling structured belief systems. The gold of truth gives you the right to examine your own sacred cows.

My clients will sometimes find a gleaming gold body-form hovering near an examination of a common belief that suddenly doesn't ring true, such as the idea that I need more friends or that my feelings are there to be hurt. I once was considering the possibility of destroying my own ego and the world it held up, and during my inner examination the archetypal image of Our Lady of Guadalupe appeared. But the rays of gold that emanated from her body turned into a horseshoe-shaped river of gold. The image, and the protective gold, stood silently behind the difficult notions that I was studying. It both reminded me that I was safe, and suggested to me that I was engaged in a truthful examination.

Another way of thinking about truth is that it's a localized representative of the vast field of objective knowledge, of all truths through all time and space. It's as if there's a field of awe engaged by truth. Truth and love are different perspectives on the same saturated, pervasive field.

When I was training to be a coach, I was told to start a client session by asking an open-ended question like "What's going on?" My job was to sit through their monologue and wait until I sensed a "landing," which could look like a pause of reflection or a sudden nervous laugh. I was to stop them then, and pursue their last statement as a possible line of inquiry.

Humans feel landings of truth. There are several definitions for intuition, describing different thought processes. I might know something is true because I've heard those words before. Or I might know something is true because my mind sorts it out quickly. Those are two ways that my mind can seem to be intuitive. But I might also know something is true because it *feels* true, as in a sensory feeling in my torso. The embodied feeling of truth usually accompanies one of the other two, brainy forms of intuition. In everyday life the embodied form of truth is rare. It's not particularly useful in a lot of circumstances, so we tend to discount its importance. If I was to rely on embodied truth, I think, I would make too many mistakes. So I ignore it to the point of forgetting that it even happens.

In spiritual work, embodied truth is less easily dismissed and might eventually seem to deserve quite a bit of attention. This is weird and to a typical rationalist sounds suspiciously unreliable. It sure did to me. I had to test it a thousand times before I was willing to grant it any province in my life.

But it's there, inside you. The gold of truth is palpable as a body-form, just as *merging love* or *strength* or *power* is. It feels both as fundamental and as ordinary as any of the other snow-globe manifestations. But in its feeling of landing, it has an extra power. Now, with truth by my side, I not only can experience *merging love* as a part of me, but I can also know that the merging love I'm experiencing is *true*. It's no longer ineffable, but solid enough to be placed into memory. Truth allows me to know that whatever I'm learning is safe and trustworthy. Truth also tells me that in some way or another I have *complete knowledge* of what has landed in me. It feels so true that I have no need to argue for its existence. I don't care a whit whether someone else finds it true.

In case you're wondering, it won't pick a horse in a race for me. It won't predict what my boss will say to me today. It won't settle any arguments with my child. It's not that kind of truth. It reserves its interests for the harder questions: Who am I? Who are you? What is it to live in a mortal body?

The body-form of truth protects my faith, and it protects my ongoing wisdom. In a way, it stops my need to second-guess myself, and so I can stay attentive to the very thing that is happening now. And now. And now.

Chapter 13

My Thin Skin

This morning I was trimming an artichoke plant in my garden, without gloves, and predictably a thorn stung me. The stems of artichoke leaves have occasional stiff hairs with sharp points that feel like splinters going in. Rose thorns puncture my skin; artichoke quills sting it.

Human beings are notorious for being thin-skinned. Unlike other large mammals, we're vulnerable to the elements in even the most temperate climates. Our mammalian brethren can roll down a rocky hill and walk away unscathed. Not us. In a way, we have to be the most cautious of mammals. And yet we don't shrink from an overmatched battle the way a coyote or lioness does. We have learned to protect our thin skins with the external tools of weaponry. With arrows or bullets, we can easily penetrate the thick skin of a lioness, long before she can sink her claws and teeth into *our* skin and sever our arteries.

The model of predator and prey that we carry in our minds sits behind the feeling of having been offended. If someone is offended by other humans' behavior too frequently, he is called "thin-skinned." Yesterday I was offended by a casual remark of my wife's. Her speech, to me, was barbed. Her sharp words took the place of the quill of my artichoke plant. This was a rare enough event that I assumed that the sharpness of the words penetrated me somehow, and hurt me. Later, I was embarrassed and noticed that I was being thin-skinned. Maybe I had even misunderstood.

We think that being offended is somehow removed from simple attack, that there is a righteous soul in us that is calling moral foul. But it's more automatic and less ethical than that. The root of "offended" is revealing in its stark assessment of its brutal nature. The word's origins go back to the verb for the simple act of striking something. Being offended is being struck, nothing more and nothing less. When I call out an offense to my self, I'm stating my simple fear of being knocked down, bruised, injured, made vulnerable, attacked.

We assume that the other person is on offense, and that our self is being attacked. By ten years old, no one really believes that it's only sticks and stones, and not words, that hurt us. Everywhere around us people are fighting back because their "pride was injured" or their "feelings were hurt." "Your words pierced my heart." "Why did you take a shot at me?" "Ouch. That was cutting." "Don't open that wound again, please." Or simply, "That hurts."

We're all thin-skinned. We all take offense. We are all hurt.

Or are we? The idea of being offended is so universal that it must be true, right? And by true we mean that it must be necessary, right?

Now take a deep breath and ask yourself some questions: "What exactly is a hurt feeling? What is hurt? Where is it hurt? What is the measurement scale for the size of the pain point or the wound? What part of it needs to be fixed? At what point is the healing done? How much of this emotional pain is real and how much of it is metaphor? If it's metaphor, what is it teaching me about reality? If it is real, what is its ideal state?"

For talking so much about hurt feelings – they're subject No. 1 for just about everyone – it's amazing how little I know about their properties or origins or measurements. The words I use for emotional bruising are obviously appropriated from physical pain, but as soon as I investigate, the metaphor tends to collapse. When my skin is pierced by a physical knife, instantly an instinctual response of nerve messages and shocked delivery of coagulants and other treatments arrive at the scene. Nothing like that happens with a hurt feeling. Sometimes it takes seconds and even minutes before the supposed barb is noticed, and often it just sits in its own dull resentment without doing a damn thing to fix itself. Could hurt feelings be imaginative creations of the mind? If so, what exactly is their danger to me? Why aren't they just pesky annoyances? Are they chimeras? Why do they stick around and build into conceptual artifacts called resentment and hatred and conflict and revenge? Have I paid much attention to this process, or have I just let it happen to me as if preordained?

Those are lots of questions to ask myself. They're hard. But there's a shortcut to finding the answers. A tool is built into you that can help you find out all about the process of taking offense. Just think back to your childhood. If you're like everybody I know, your sense of personal outrage is stored compactly and efficiently in two or three stories of childhood – traumatic memories, they're called – that are your bugbears and, paradoxically, your keys to the kingdom.

My client Sonya was born in Stalin's Russia. She remembers the dangerous time – she was six or seven – when her father, a university professor with an impeccable revolutionary past, nevertheless was in mortal peril and carefully, secretly, got the family to safety in England. She recollects well the danger while they were on the run, and the need to be especially quiet and obedient. She recalls being told how to answer officials and what not to say. But those are remembered as interesting events, even daring times, and they carry little emotional charge beyond the joy of curiosity and storytelling. What Sonya evokes more frequently and with dread to this day is her classmates at her new school in England. Because of her strange language and clothes, Sonya the new kid was bullied and kept an outcast by the other girls. In particular, she recalls a girl named Kate at a birthday party taking the hem of Sonya's satin-ribboned, flocked Russian dress and spinning her around while sarcastically singing a maypole song. Sonya carries the humiliation with her to this day.

All of us have our wrong dress, wrong-way-of-being stories of childhood humiliation. They may be buried under a sprinkling of soil. The trick is to find them, scrape off the soil, and examine them repeatedly. Is this *the* story of my childhood, or one of many? If there are many, including times of delight, then why is this one so prominent? Eventually you might find that your memories are inclined to be negative and that the strongest ones are of shame. The lesson being instilled is something like this:

"Beware of shame, and spend lots of time protecting myself from it." Something in you keeps reminding you of this, and keeps your wrong dress story lurking slightly underground. You notice that your memories are curated. You might wonder who curates them, and for what purpose?

We'll return to this, but for now it's just helpful to notice how much of life is spent in protection from being offended, which, in turn, protects us from possible humiliation.

The idea that we might not be shameful beings – and might not need to protect ourselves from having shame exposed – does not occur to most of us. Fortunately, there are a number of internal supports – body-forms – that encourage us to see past our belief that the world is about to attack us for who we are, shame us, offend us. These supports don't deny the attack; they just provide us with knowledge that the attack can't actually hurt us.

Forgiveness

We've already discussed compassion – the form of love that arises in the presence of suffering. Forgiveness is a mechanical offshoot from compassion. While compassion is a field, forgiveness is more of a situational tool that clears the way for compassion and other qualities. Jesus tells me to forgive and even to love my enemy. Sunday School and kindergarten teachers say the same thing. My so-called friends and family commit unforgivable injuries that others ask me to forgive. How do I do that? What's in it for me?

Forgiveness is my inbuilt ability to accept hurt feelings and emotional offenses as annoyances rather than damage. When I think I have been damaged by someone else's offensive remark, I'm mistaking my personality for my broader, true self. When I'm aware that my value isn't dependent on how someone treats me, my hurt feelings dissipate. This isn't being good, a moral form of forgiveness. I don't forgive because I'm supposed to, grudgingly. This is the lighthearted feeling that I am free of grudges.

Regrettably, this kind of forgiveness is absolute. I don't get to pick or choose whom to forgive. I've solved the root of forgiveness – the mistake that annoyances and disrespect can damage me. I forgive the family member who constantly tells me what's wrong with me with the same alacrity as I do the absent-minded driver whose car hit a puddle and splashed me. This kind of forgiveness is absolute; once it settles in, revenge stops being of interest.

As a body-form, forgiveness feels weightless, clean and soft, and it shines turquoise. When the turquoise presence arrives, it has its own wisdom and freshness. It's so much easier not to carry grudges, and not to worry about hurt feelings. The annoying offenses have a way of passing through the body without stopping to imagine themselves being attached to the heart or belly or brain. Have you ever met a schoolyard bully later in life, and noticed how small they now seemed?

Acceptance

Sometimes the issue isn't that you're bearing a grudge but that things are just going wrong, and you feel crummy. It might be no one's fault. You planned to spend the day at the lake, but it's raining. A friend died. You returned from two weeks on the road to a garden out of control with weeds, dead spots, and collapsing plants. No matter how many times you rewrote the sentence, it didn't come out right.

Life is frustrating and out of kilter in hundreds of ways, every day. Each time your control and predictive ability are questioned, you are given the chance to collapse emotionally, or at least kick the dirt and complain.

It turns out to be a false assumption that things are supposed to be a certain way. They're only supposed to be the way they are. Sometimes that's not convenient. Acceptance is the recognition that I'm always OK starting from where I am, and I don't ever need to start from where I would rather be.

Acceptance has a feeling of contentment without needing any specific object of contentment. Like the turquoise of forgiveness, the aquamarine of acceptance has a way of showing up just as a color, saturating your interior or some part of a scene that is already being highlighted. Examined closely, the color also exhibits a lightness and crystalline twinkle. It represents the way of not trying to correct the world as it is unfolding. The world will always organize itself on its own terms, and when you take it as it is, your actions will be sharper, more accurate and more loving. Paradoxically, acceptance doesn't deny free will. It provides a healthier, more relaxed and complete base for the change that you want to create.

Surrender

Sometimes, however, free will has to be surrendered. When I'm not just disliking what is – the rain, the death, the unkempt garden, the words on the page – but I'm also berating God for making it this way, then I might need stronger medicine.

Surrender takes me all the way to a place of non-resistance. I give up on fixing things myself. I give up on good ideas. I give up on thinking I am capable of making a difference. I even give up on acceptance of what is. I stand still and let the world revolve around me, and I notice what is changing in me as surrender sinks in.

The feeling is one of melting honey, dark gold, not just soaking through my troubles but annihilating them from top to bottom. The honey becomes part of me as I give in to the divine. I'm not fighting the world. Nor am I withdrawing from the world. I'm here, in my location, powerless for the moment because my eyes are on the elegant workings of an unknowable divine. I'm humble. My ego has receded for now. I might notice some long-held structures become porous, at least for the moment. It's OK for me to be undefended; surrender implies faith in the divine, or at least in an accurate portrayal of what is. Experiencing it for a moment or two doesn't damage my chance to express free will next.

Vulnerability

Finally, through encounters with forgiveness, acceptance, and surrender, I come to perceive my own vulnerability as a divine aspect of God. I've seen how being thin-skinned emotionally takes me into dramas of the personality that are neither necessary nor helpful. I've seen that I have substantial supports inside me that make my defenses seem childish and flimsy.

Being thin-skinned turns out to be a good thing. We know it to be objectively true that humans are physically thin-skinned, materially less prepared for the world than other large mammals. Our brains need the calories and energy that other animals use to create their thick hides.

Once humans are accustomed to their lack of protective coating, they get better and better at prospering through ingenuity – the work of their brains and self-reflection – rather than armor. In a similar fashion, it is objectively true that I am emotionally thin-skinned, emotionally less prepared for the world than large mammals that lack the ability to second-guess themselves. Once I'm accustomed to my emotional penetrability, I use ingenuity to turn that penetrability into a new, strong form of vulnerability.

We're told a false story that vulnerability leaves us weak. Actually, our ingenuity, our ability to second-guess ourselves, our self-reflection – whatever you want to call the peculiarly human way of thinking – are our superpowers. The hidebound creatures are limited in their resourcefulness. Vulnerability yields objective consideration. We can't rely on impulsive, instinctual reaction like our large mammalian brethren. We're too vulnerable for that. We find a higher level of planning and thinking. We trade physical strength for the strength that relies on careful and objective discrimination, and we discover judo, the way of using dispassionate thought to get our way. Emotions stop our thoughts before they've reached objectivity; releasing the emotions, letting them pass through us, opens up new possibilities.

The body-form of vulnerability is water. Ali doesn't call this body-form vulnerability. He calls it water. He describes it as humanness. He considers vulnerability a kind of subset of the water form. I like to use the term vulnerability because of the irony, that what we come to learn as a weakness turns out to be the word corresponding to a wonderful quality of the divine.

As a human, it turns out, I'm not so much a heavy solid. I'm more like water – transparent, clean, simple, penetrable, shapeshifting, conforming to nature, ever-falling, flowing, breakable into like parts called drops that rejoin to form rivers and oceans. As water, I contain things that aren't me, touch things that aren't me, but spend most of my time in an aggregate that can be seen to be moving on its own power at the same time that it's clearly propelled without resistance. Water is paradoxically related to nothingness, or just the bare scant nature of being, and to the juice of life, necessary and elemental.

Gratitude

I'll close this section on our human, thin-skinned properties with a brief mention of the body-form gratitude, which is peculiar in that it's the only body-form that looks to the past. All the other thirty-four body-forms are firmly rooted in the present. Whatever emotional issue has drawn you to the body-form, it usually wipes out your belief about what happened and lands you squarely in the present. Gratitude isn't like that. It keeps you looking at the past, and asks you to find the hidden treasure that is contained in memory.

In a way it doesn't belong in this chapter. While forgiveness, acceptance, surrender and vulnerability all clear the way for the next experience, gratitude tends to be a quality of an experience that I'm having for its own sake. I stop for a moment of appreciation. It isn't necessarily related to what's coming next.

Here's a radical notion: What if tears are always gratitude? What if the anguish side of grief and loss are shadowy artifacts of civilization, while tears are the authentic recognition of how useful or wonderful someone has been in my life? I can't prove this, but I toy with it. Today a client of mine was examining her busy need to stay popular, a near-universal side effect of living among strangers who distrust each other. She was recognizing that the hamster wheel of popularity leaves little concern or room for being alone, engaged in self-study or reading. She remembered herself as a kid loving to withdraw from the world and dive into novels, one after another. She started to tear up, and as she came out of the trance she made a self-deprecating comment, as if her tears were a scabrous self-pity.

I found myself sternly telling her to take a moment and look past her notions of tears being sorrow, and instead notice how she had acknowledged and felt compassion for the self who had lost sight of withdrawal and aloneness and their lovely way of being. What's so sad about being a softy? What's so sad about appreciating simplicity?

Gratitude always appreciates. I don't know why that is. It isn't the appreciation of the sacrifice of the other, which is how we're taught gratitude. "She didn't have to do that for you, so thank her." It's simpler than that. It's appreciation that such a person was in my life once upon a time, and a vague notice of the lessons and support that came along with that person. I feel gratitude for my mother's schizoaffective disorder, not out of pity for her or out of a sense of filial duty but because I know it brought interests to me that led to wonders that include writing this book. "If not for her mental illness ..." becomes "Thanks to her mental illness ..."

While forgiveness, acceptance, surrender, and vulnerability all allow me to see beyond my judgment that something is undesirable, and find what's really there instead, gratitude reminds me that my litany of judgments are questionable and at best trivial. If I have somehow missed the light in the world, I have no one else to blame. It has all been given to me for my use.

As usual, I need to point out that this isn't pollyannish or solipsistic. It is simply recognizing my small place in an otherwise unfathomable interdependence of things. Sometimes that is quite helpful to me. At other times, I am squarely footed in politics, religion, or some other mechanical system that intercedes with help for my natural distrust of the strangers in my life. And when I am participating in a political system, I give myself up to the ethical code – the restraints of human law – and apply myself to justice and fairness. Lightly. But I might also notice that *justice* and *fairness* aren't found among the thirty-five divine body-forms. They don't describe parts of the essence of me. They are socially relevant restraints on my actions in a world of strangers.

Chapter 14

But Who Am I?

A few years ago I visited an ashram in Southern India devoted to Ramana Maharshi, a guru who died there in 1950. My friend Meg, whom I met in the 1980s when we were both reporters at a New Jersey newspaper, has lived near the ashram for fifteen years. Now that I was on my own spiritual path, she insisted that I come visit. Most of my days I spent on the ashram grounds; nights were in the spare dormitory across the street. I ate communal meals on the floor with food slopped onto banana leaves, sat around and meditated, observed daily Hindu ceremonies, hung out nearby with Meg, spent a cold, windy night at the rocky top of the sacred mountain overlooking the ashram, and concentrated repeatedly on the being and messages of Ramana Maharshi. His path can be summed up as a lifelong pursuit of a single question: "Who am I?"

I also began the research for this book. At the time I was most interested in linking the body-forms to the philosophy of Plato. The plan for the book was to tie the body-forms closely to Plato's notion of inborn ideals. Does a person already know what "the good" is, before finding it in morality and their own actions, as Plato had said they did? Were we born with an imbedded vocabulary? I thought so, and wondered whether these body-forms of Hameed Ali were a missing link to what Plato had been talking about. In pursuing this line of questioning, I also needed some grounding in modern linguistics, to study the bridges between words, body-forms, concepts, and things. It turned out that the ashram had a lovely new library, and in the stacks I discovered some beat-up copies of the Socratic dialogues and a recent textbook on linguistics, donated by previous visitors. Bingo!

I lived temporarily in three lives: the explorer of self, the productive scholar, and the familiar friend. The first two were solitary endeavors, one less worldly than the other, and the third was both interpersonal and worldly.

I can explore myself. I can explore the world. I can explore my relationship with people in the world. In the first two, I am looking for an answer to *what is true?* In the third, I am asking instead *what is love?*

Most of the divine body-objects are in service to how we humans interact with the outside world. Hidden in that statement is the idea that there's a *me* who experiences *that*. The mystery of the *me*, the *that*, and their *relationship* to each other give us theology, philosophy, psychology, anthropology, and sociology, plus all the other sciences. They give us Ramana Maharshi and his question, *Who am I?* Most of the divine body-forms help give me a clearer view of the *other,* or how to see through my subjective interpretation of life into an objective view of my relations with others. But two of them give me a direct view of myself, the *me* involved in this thing called life.

Fittingly, one of them, which Ali calls The Pearl, is focused on the relational side of life – our commitment to each other, to shared activities, to play and productivity. The other, which he calls The Point, is focused on the observational side of life – our sense of awe in nature, our ability to see ourselves as a drop in the ocean, our capacity for pure objectivity.

I think of the Point as the place where truth unfolds and the Pearl as the place where love unfolds. Life isn't as cleanly separated as that, but it's helpful to first discriminate the two before seeing how they might blend together.

The Point

Self-discovery boils down to the question of how I continue the sentence that begins "I am ..." When I ask my clients, "Who are you?" they typically respond, "I am a mother. I am a kind person. I am a thoughtful person. I am a lesbian. I am sometimes mean. I am a wife. I am ethnic Chinese. I am a lawyer." And on and on. These are called roles or identities. They are fixed notions of what distinguishes me from the mass of people around me. They are actually answering the question, "What about you distinguishes you from others?" Each identity carries with it a sense of where I fit in, or what my purpose is as viewed by others.

We have a seemingly inexhaustible supply of identities. Tiny differentiations show up as fixed identities. "I'm a person who likes chocolate ice cream" can be an identity, especially if you are amazed that you share the planet with people who dislike chocolate. "I can't imagine living without chocolate" is said with a notion of truth alongside the obvious hyperbole. We subsequently feel a kinship with fellow chocolate lovers, and a sense of separation from people who avoid the taste of chocolate. When we add up all the big and small differentiations – all of our identities – we think we have individuated ourselves. And that sense of uniqueness gives us a social personhood that can toggle between feeling accepted and feeling apart.

I become self-defined by all my identities, which are built to join or separate from the pack. We'll call this way of looking at ourselves our personality, our way of being a (unique) person in the world.

No client has yet blurted out, "I am a human being" during this exercise. It's as if the base on which all these identities exist doesn't matter much.

But just as a flower or wolf is something without its having a sense of its differentiated identity, so are we humans. With flowers and wolves we share the ubiquitous characteristics of life force, development and maturation, death, survival skills, respiration, sensory organs, and an organizing principle. We are fascinated by how these basic structures operate in other creatures. For ourselves? They are seldom interesting except insofar as we can overcome them through medicine and science.

We do have one faculty that other living creatures seem to lack: self-reflection. But we don't employ it as much as we think, or in the way that we think we do. We oddly subvert our singular gift by focusing narrowly on what is different about each of us, and paying scant attention to what is common. We don't reflect on our most obvious, simple characteristics.

But repeatedly asking "Who am I?" – the ultimate question of self-reflection – eventually draws our universal nature into focus. Eventually we notice that an almost unbearably simple base supports all of our chosen identities. If I notice that being a father or worker or scold or friend is a choice, then I start to wonder what *me* is making that choice. At first the base looks empty, as if deficiency is its only characteristic, as if the *me* who makes identity choices operates without any internal principles or mooring. *Me* without my roles and identities seems like nothing. This is commonly felt as depression. As my clients work with me, experiencing the body-forms, they often encounter a sudden realization that they have no idea who is running the show. With this deficient emptiness comes a listless feeling, malaise, thoughts of meaninglessness and hopelessness, and a troubled worry that that's all there is: nothing much. All these feelings and thoughts are normal. They also seem to be necessary – for varying lengths of time – before breaking through to the actual fundamental platform on which your active human life rests. The sense of depression requires the misunderstanding that I'm not made of the things the body-forms represent, when I am. I learn that I'm not who I thought I was, but I also learn that I have all the same divine characteristics as everyone else.

This "Who am I?" process isn't linear. It isn't mapped out for you. It requires persistent questioning of your basic beliefs. It's harrowing at times; who wants to feel listless and lacking, even knowing that it might be a temporary passage? But exploring deficiency does have its rewards. Jesus described this process as the first Beatitude: Blessed are the poor in spirit. Getting poor in spirit is the process of stripping away the personality, all of my notions that being liked, being rich, being holy, being helpful, being wise, being famous, being better than others, being noticed, having a packed-house memorial service, being creative, being altruistic, being dominant, or being subservient will get me into heaven. Heaven, by the way, is here on earth, so if you haven't noticed it around you, then what you've been trying probably hasn't worked.

Sometimes this deficient emptiness can be felt as an emptiness in the belly, or as an empty column running from your head down to your seat. But there's another form it takes that precedes an experience of the Point. It might take a couple of years for it to make an appearance, but I'm mentioning it here because it's a tipping point that deserves to be noticed. First the false self of identities and roles appears as a bean-shaped object in my client's lower left abdomen. That bean or pea is a dry, shrunken representation of the entire personality. It is who you think you are as an individuated person, and by sitting with it, who you really are – an explorer of truth – can eventually show up.

When the client has studied her identities enough – how long varies enormously – the pea may disappear and the experience of the Point may happen.

My clients commonly experience the Point like this: The back wall of their torso opens up to a night sky. It's deep, shiny black. Stars and galaxies appear, but not in the common dome that we see when looking up at night. Instead this night sky opens up as space, and the client notices that she can will herself as a traveler through space, as if she is her own spaceship. The stars and galaxies are approachable. The passing heavenly bodies don't generally differentiate – they remain far enough away as to appear like the twinkly stars do to the naked eye – but the near-endless space can be traversed at leisure.

The Point is me without my surfaces, my beliefs, and my identities. I become an infinitesimal point – little more than a location with eyes – watching the awesome splendor of everything around me. Without the baggage of my beliefs, I am objective. I also become aware of simple fascination and how it underlies my sense of what is true. The field I am in is one of objective reality, or truth. I'm scarcely part of it, except for my ability to register it and appreciate it.

The Point answers *two* critical questions for me, it turns out: "Who am I?" and "What is true nature?"

The Pearl

If the Point represents my fundamental relationship with truth, then the Pearl opens my parallel association with love. In the attitude of the Point, "Who am I?" led to *truth* as we explored our questionable concepts. The same question leads to *love* as we see through our emotional fixations.

The Pearl answers, "Who am I – in relation to other human beings?"

As I encounter my emotional difficulties one by one through a body-form exercise, they first appear as individual objects in my body, offering themselves up for inquiry. Each may give way to a divine body-form. But eventually I encounter a lot of them at once, and they coalesce into a broad sense of deficient emptiness – a vacant sphere in the belly or hollow column down the center of my body. These represent the failure of my belief that externalities – money, fame, power, or even just one more friend – will finally make me happy. The more I explore my beliefs in my own striving and see how they never yield sustained satisfaction, the more likely they are to collapse into a deficient emptiness. It is not uncommon for a client of mine to hit a tipping point that takes her into an uncomfortable depression for weeks or months. Unfortunately, the way out of suffering is through examination of the suffering. It has to rid itself through being examined. But every one of my clients has emerged with something new – solid rather than deficient, unified rather than separated – and seemingly permanent.

Ultimately this journey takes them to their true self, the Pearl that can be experienced as knowing yourself as a ball of love. That's who I actually am as a person in the world who relates to other people.

In the Point, I am a passive observer. In the Pearl, I am a dynamic participant. Most of my work through the Big Five body-forms – curiosity, strength, will, compassion, and power – is leading me straight to the Pearl. The Pearl is the basis for all my activity in the world. I'm seeing myself as an active human, whose curiosity morphs into worldly action and results in connection with my cellular self and with others who share a similar cellular self. At the barest level of action, I'm feeding myself and others, sheltering myself and others, and clothing myself and others. These are participatory necessities for the survival of my body and the collective body of my species.

The Pearl appears unexpectedly, usually as a white sphere, as small as a pearl or as large as a torso. It has the white of milk and the same opalescence. It might seem thin and airy or thick and liquid. As my client concentrates on it, it often expands like a balloon beyond the skin and into the external world a ways. Or it may stay inside but fill every inch of the client's body. It is simple and white and lively.

Some people find their Pearl before examining the deficient emptiness, and others afterward. But seeing it isn't knowing it to be fundamental. To fully integrate it, to come to the belief that it is who they are essentially, and that it is capable of leading them through a functioning life, seems to require a full descent into the particulars of their suffering. Maybe it is introduced beforehand to let the seeker get a glimpse of the reward at the end of their work. I don't know, but often visions work this way. Integrating the Point and the Pearl is hard work.

The Pearl turns out to be both a thing in itself – roughly comparable to the soul – and also a container for any support I might need. So the Pearl can fill my body with redness if I need strength, or yellowness if I need curiosity. It is simple, but carries all my potential interests and activities, too, especially those that involve human beings. That means it is available when I am at work in an office, after work having drinks with my friends, in bed with my partner, and alone with my tears. It is the basic me who interacts with others, and also the me who is interested in myself.

For most of my clients, it is a relief to discover their Pearl, and it also provides an acceptable answer to two questions: "Who am I?" and "What is my soul?"

Shapes of Truth

Chapter 15

❧ ❧

Other Aspects of God

You have been introduced to half of the entire set of divine body-forms. You can find these and the remaining ones at the back of the book, in a catalog with tips that help you interpret them when they appear in your own body. Now, though, it's time to learn how to evoke them in yourself. They're mere words on a page so far, but their magic is that they're better, purer than words.

My clients and most fellow students of Ali don't experience all thirty-five of them, let alone engage many of them long enough for them to become an easily accessible part of us. We don't need to. A few will do. The divine body-forms serve two purposes: to show up episodically in you as a support for an immediate difficulty, and to help you discover who you actually are and what your soul and mind harmonize with. To engage those two purposes, most people need to discover only six or eight divine body-forms well enough that they feel integrated into their normal functioning. The Big Five are prominent for just about everyone, and then often one or two or three of the other ones I've presented so far. Get to that point, and you've progressed to such an understanding of them that this book may be of little or no use to you anymore.

We're about to swerve from concepts into technique. But the attitude is the same: open-minded inquiry.

One of my favorite things about accidentally entering a spiritual path late in life is that, surprisingly, I didn't have to give up the pattern recognition and logic skills that I developed so assiduously early in life. These were the brain-tools that had gotten me jobs, helped me raise children, and kept me up to date with my Apple and Microsoft products. When encountering the body-forms, I'm just applying those same brain skills to different material. My new intellectual territory encounters the material of the soul, I guess, or at least that's my current wording.

The body-forms have an internal logic and an applicability to real life that can be rich and soul-searching, while their appearance and dynamics are simpler. Instead of jarring, the body-forms themselves are easygoing and nonconfrontational. Yes, the experiences with body-forms have a way of granting me admission to pure forms of awe and love. Yes, they're spectacularly crystalline in how they cut through to a richer reality. But they're not disruptive; they're additive. They don't replace what I already have discovered. They're just more.

Think of it this way: You can have two vocabularies now. One you grew up with. It's the vocabulary of the little nagging voice inside you and includes such words as *productive, abused, worthless, loved, achieving, lazy, happy, sad, threatened, hated, just, fair, unfair,* and *crazy.* I could list hundreds more of its words, but you get the point. To whom is that little nagging voice talking? What if the person it is talking to has a much smaller, even rudimentary, vocabulary of thirty-five words? What if they are words such as *curiosity, strength, power, love,* and *value*? What if they're the only concepts that the core self needs to know in order to describe itself? What if they're an antidote to misery?

Shapes of Truth

Chapter 16

You Can Do It

Anyone can have experiences of the body-forms. Anyone. It just takes a little concentration, and the help of a friend. Don't believe me? Try it. Here are the steps:

- Find a quiet place, where you and your friend can concentrate. I've done it walking in the woods, but usually in two chairs, facing each other.

- You ask the questions. The friend who will have the experience answers. First ask the friend to think about an emotional concern from the previous few hours, something bugging them that triggered an unpleasant feeling. Tell the friend that you don't need to know what it was.

- Now ask your friend to close their eyes and mentally look into their torso, the space between their chin and legs. Ask whether they notice anything different, a spot where there's heat or pressure, or a flutter, or anything. Ignore chronic pain, injury symptoms, or GI disturbances. You're looking for something a little more subtle.

 → The friend will tell you what they've found. It will often be a feeling of pressure or constriction. Your attitude is one of focus detached from judgment. You're a scientist proceeding carefully through an experiment.

→ Repeat back to your friend what they said. Simplify it if need be, but don't add anything, and don't try to explain it. Let's say the friend responded, "There's a kind of warm spot, I don't know, kind of heat, in the area below my ribcage." You might say back to them, "You're feeling warmth in your solar plexus. Right?"

→ Always agree with whatever they describe, and repeat it back. It's helpful to visualize the object yourself, in the subject's torso. When there's an opening for you, ask the following questions about their feeling, generally in this order:

  o How wide is it?

  o How tall is it?

  o How thick is it?

  o Does it have a shape or is it a blob?

  o Is it attached to anything?

  o Does it have a color?

  o What is its density? Airy, liquid, hard, rubbery, wooden, metal?

   ∾ Accumulate the characteristics as you go. Let's say you've gotten to Question 5. You: "Is it attached to anything, or is it floating?" The friend responds, "It feels like it's in space, and it's just kind of hanging there." You: "So you have a sphere six inches in diameter floating in space in the area of your solar plexus, right?" Friend: "Yes." You: "What color is it?"

   ∾ Once you've gone through all the questions, invite your friend to continue to notice and examine the object. Remind them to be interested only in its physical characteristics, not how it got there or what it represents. "So you have a brown sphere six inches in diameter floating in space in the area of your solar plexus, and its interior is like brown smoke, and its exterior has a rubbery skin. Now just pay attention to it, and let me know if anything changes."

What is this? The experience that your friend has is not like anything else in life, except maybe dreaming. What business would an imaginary object have in your torso during your waking life? Peculiarly, the person experiencing the object typically has a matter-of-fact belief in it. None of the normal apparatus of distrust toward an irrational experience appears. My completely non-spiritual, non-religious, atheistic, rationalistic friends and relatives accept the presence of the imaginary body in exactly the same attitude as my most woo-woo friends. It's weird, that. It's as if all judgment is suspended – for anyone – during the experience.

That's the point. Judgment takes a holiday.

Each time you do this, a different object may appear. Most objects first appear as simple blobs, spheres, oblongs or empty columns. The practice example of a brown sphere filled with gas is typical.

When engaged in this exercise, the subject often notices two successive body-forms, with a long, empty pause between them. Both are true, but the first usually represents suffering and the second a divine aspect of God.

The first form that shows up in the body typically represents the emotional task on the person's mind. Conjuring up the pictured form in the torso replaces the mental activity of trying to fix or deal with or deny what's wrong – the preference to change or move away from negative things. If the friend starts by recalling a bout of jealousy, the first body-form she finds might represent the feeling of being unloved and the desire to be loved again. If the person starts with worry about work, the object might represent the desire to quit procrastinating.

Most people I know avoid thinking too much about concepts like feeling unloved, or jealous, or overwhelmed by work. When I'm in avoidance, I'm unconsciously adopting the position that by dwelling on negative representations of myself (I am not lovable, I am slothful), I'll feel pain, or reinforce the negative belief, or I'll start a downward slide through my stated deficiency all the way to catastrophe.

So I engage in strategies of avoidance, telling myself to buck up and ignore these negative emotions. Even the best of us do this. You know who you are.

But no matter how successful my strategy of avoidance may seem at first, I soon encounter further gnawing thoughts about the sensed deficiency that started the whole thing. The jealousy or work anxiety leaks back in, and I am again enervated. This is the pathetic Groundhog Day of the monkey mind.

The body-form exercise offers a reprieve from all that. These body-forms perform a simple, helpful task for us. They allow us to concentrate on our specific plight with attention, focus, and curiosity. What is this strange object in me? Giving myself a few minutes of uninterrupted attention to a representation of the plight seems to free me – albeit temporarily – from much sense of suffering. In the body-form representation of my plight, it can receive a thoroughly objective going-over. I'm not questioning it; I'm accepting it. It's just an imaginary brown sphere. That can't hurt me, right? I'm not thinking words like "jealousy" or "work anxiety." I'm thinking words like "brown sphere." They're neutral. Without a name, it doesn't have to be avoided, because it's not alarming. In a way, the object is seen for what it is, without the usual judgments supplied by my active mind and without my frantic desire to run away before seeing it completely.

This is a marvel in itself, but it's nothing compared with the marvel that follows.

Let's resume the inquiry with your friend. When the friend has completely established the characteristics of the body-form, his or her final task is simply to stay attentive to it. It's not time to stop yet. Your only job here is to keep your friend focused. We're not used to staying attentive to a simple object that isn't changing. For as much as five minutes, the object will just sit there, being watched.

And then!

Usually you'll notice a slight look of surprise on your friend's face. "What was that?" you ask.

"It's moving."

"Where's it moving?"

The first body-form, the one that represents suffering, moves in one of five ways. It can simply shrink and dissipate, and if attention is kept on it, shrink all the way to non-existence or dissipate totally into the general torso. Or it can seem to fly out of the body from where it is, struggling a little before poking out through the skin. Or it can slowly push its way up toward the throat and then out the mouth. Or it can slide or melt down into a pool at the bottom of the stomach and then shrink to nothing. Or it can move up through the body and depart through an opening in the top of the head.

Make sure that your friend stays attentive to the moving object all the way through its disappearance. Ask questions like, "Where's it going? Is it gone? Did it make it all the way out?" If it stops pushing out and reconstitutes itself, then stay with the new form of the suffering object. Start the first set of questions over again. Eventually it will push all the way out.

Then you both just sit and wait for what's next. The suffering body-form is gone. Tell your friend to focus on the now-empty spot where the body-object used to reside. Ask your friend how they feel. This is the one time when it's worthwhile to temporarily remove the friend's attention from the body-object location.

"How do you feel?"

Typically, the friend notices a funny feeling of contentment, often accompanied by a grin. The friend says something like, "I feel OK, no, not just OK, but it's like *everything's* OK." A sense of general and complete well-being will have supplanted the suffering that provoked the body-form.

Now guide your friend back to the torso.

"But it's empty now," the friend might say.

"Yes, it's empty. Just pay attention to the emptiness."

If the friend doesn't come up with anything new after a minute or two, you can ask them what color the back wall of their torso is.

With or without that prompting, the friend may sit up and say something like, "That's odd."

"What's odd?"

"There's a white sphere in my stomach," the friend will say. Or: "I've got a sense of my head opening up." Or: "Everything's turning red with flecks of gold." Or any of hundreds of possibilities.

It is at this point that your friend has started to experience a divine interior presence, one or more of the thirty-five pure aspects of God. The white sphere? The body-form for personal essence, the Pearl, your true self without ego. The head opening up? The body-form for guidance or clarity, the ability to discriminate truth accurately. The red with flecks of gold? Your built-in strength, mixed with your built-in capacity to know the truth.

So there are two kinds of body-forms. There are ones that can represent what we're thinking about, or worried about, or trying to fix. They have recognizable characteristics, which reveal that they are not representative of ideals, but of the truth of an illusory notion we might have, or the truth that we wish we could get rid of something that we feel is debasing us. And there is a specific set of thirty-five pure and simple body-forms that represent essential aspects of the divine.

Don't take my word for it. Go out and try a body-form exercise with a friend. This is an experiential process, and it just plain doesn't work conceptually.

I wish you could do this alone right from the start. But experience with clients has shown that it's just too hard at first.

Shapes of Truth

What Just Happened To Me?

I magine that God or the divine or the absolute is a many-faceted gem. Each facet is a different color – primary colors and blended colors, red and white and orange and pomegranate and on and on. Each colored facet is a divine characteristic of God – an aspect of God. Each facet also is a word in the language of the beholder. In English there's a red facet that represents "strength," a white facet that represents "will," an orange facet that represents "pleasure," a pomegranate facet that represents "passion," and on and on, thirty-five of these.

What do you say when you peer closely at a gem? You say that you're looking *into* it. In the analogy, any one of the colored facets doesn't just exhibit a color of the divine but it also provides a visual entryway to the core of the divine, and opens up every other color that is blending its way to the focal point. And then there's the focal point itself: another, slightly different representation of the absolute itself.

So "strength" has an existence as a word in the English language, as a meaning in a dictionary, as a solid body in the realm of the forms (a ruby), as an essential aspect, as a color (red) that distinguishes it as an essential aspect, as an entryway to the divine, as a quality of the divine, as an object that contributes to transformation, and as a participation in divinity that can be integrated into everyday consciousness.

And you thought strength just meant being physically or mentally capable of getting what you wanted!

It still means that, but when encountered in the realm of the forms, as an essential aspect, it accumulates a capacity for action in a rather perfect way.

In my everyday life, strength often arises with a feeling of steeling myself, making myself stronger. It is the result of lifting weights, or preparing for a test, or telling myself to stand up for myself. In this everyday form of strength, I think of myself as a vessel that needs to be filled to be defended. I better have some available strength or I'll lose, or fall, or fail, or get hurt. If I don't have enough strength, I'm in trouble. Left to my own devices, unprepared, without strengthening, maybe I'm weak. Maybe on balance I have more weakness than strength. Uh-oh. Can I? Maybe I can't.

The body-form feeling of strength isn't like that. It isn't the result of hard work; it is available always, complete in itself. It doesn't trigger a memory of weakness. It doesn't need to steel itself, get itself ready, or replace a weak notion with a strong one. It isn't on a search for resources. It needs no replenishment.

Essential strength is like a substance that just shows up and exhibits itself. It's always there. It might provide what I need in the moment, or it might just let me know what it is so I can trust that it will arrive when needed.

And it isn't just for arm-wrestling. The feeling of strength – what we often call confidence – is more the result of correctly evaluating and discriminating what the challenge is about and less about bluster and pumping up.

The point of strength isn't so much to shout out, "I can!" as it is to let me know just what my true capacity is. The strongest thing to do when overmatched might be to walk away and wait for a better opening. We use the word courage for strength of heart. And the strength of the heart is its ability to assess the obstacle accurately and respond appropriately. As a body-form it is red. As a feeling it is energetic, full-blooded and heartfelt.

Each of the thirty-five essential aspects is like that. It has its false form and its true form. I'll often engage the false form because I don't believe that the true form is available. Take another essential aspect, compassion: I might believe that at heart I'm selfish and that I should be kind instead, and so I pretend to be compassionate. I may have learned to act compassionately so well that I don't even notice anymore that there's a fear of selfishness lurking, but if I examine myself closely, it's there. As long as the compassion feels at all shaky, as if it needed support, I know it isn't the true compassion, which is unwilled and ever-present.

Or take will. It was one of the first of the thirty-five that I experienced in its full-fledged body-form. This was a decade ago, when I was in a spiritual group that studied the body-forms.

I sat on a chair facing a friend in a large room. Other paired-off people were sprinkled around the room. My tongue ran on in a monologue covering my history of procrastination. Why did I put so much off? Was it fear of failure? Fear of success? Fear of being small? Fear of being big? Oh, my, so many procrastinations: my chores, my work, my hopes, my dreams, my tasks, my goals. I stopped. Downcast, my attention turned in to my body. This was in 2010, but it might as well have been ten years earlier, or thirty years. I was struggling with a lifelong shadow.

All of a sudden my back straightened, and a rush of vibration swept up my spine. What spine? Instead of a spine, I experienced a platinum bar an inch wide and a quarter inch thick running from my coccyx up to my cranium. This foreign object had replaced my spine! What the hell? As I experienced it, and kept my attention on it, the bar gleamed white-silver and seemed to settle into my own contentment. I felt alive, alert, and refreshed. I stopped talking about procrastination, and fell into a casual conversation with my friend.

The feeling of the platinum bar puzzled me. It clearly was imaginary; my spine is a physical part of me that carves a bony stripe on X-rays. But the platinum bar didn't *feel* unreal. It didn't feel like a thought, or as if it had been constructed by my imagination. I didn't stop believing that I'm skin and bones and maybe a little fat here or there, or that no platinum bar would show up on an X-ray.

I stored the odd experience away in memory.

A few years later I was in the same room, this time listening to a lecture. The teacher that day, Florentin Krause, spoke in a soft, German-accented voice about willpower, and the feeling of being irresolute. All of us nodded along as he described procrastination. He talked about the feeling of going to war with our desire to avoid unwelcome or difficult tasks, how we try to summon up willpower to get over the hump. And then he described a capacity to tap into a deeper source of will – a universal will that is constantly pervading us and the world, and that can respond to any task with alacrity. All of it sounded a bit abstract.

He ended the lecture with a call for us to meditate.

After we settled in, he guided us. At some point he said, "Now imagine that your spine has been replaced by a platinum bar."

A jolt went up my ... spine!

It turns out that the body-form of "universal will" – the abstract concept represented by the two words – is also represented by a color, an element, and a solid body that can be sought and found. This was one of my first experiences with one of the full-fledged objects found in the body. How could this happen?

Recall that it first appeared as false will, or what is known as willpower. My inquiry began with my belief that I didn't have enough willpower. That was the problem at hand. "What's wrong with me? Why can't I get things done efficiently like other people? Why do I procrastinate? I don't like this about myself." It was only after exploring that thoroughly that the true universal will appeared as a platinum bar replacing my spine.

The false form of an essential aspect is usually wrapped in a belief that I lack easy access to a capacity that others have. I think of myself as a container that isn't full. I believe that I have to add some *oomph* to myself in order to succeed. In the case of willpower, I have to fix my lack of willpower and get things done. I try things on: "Maybe a schedule will work. Maybe nagging myself will work. Maybe willing my willpower will work." They're all things that I have to *do*. I want a tool, and I need to supply it to myself or something bad will happen. I think to myself that otherwise something shameful, like sloth, will happen. And I tell myself that when sloth is allowed to fester, I lose my ability to succeed and survive. I can always tell when a false form of an aspect has arisen, because it comes with a sense of conflict, a nagging voice, and anxiety.

In the example of my first encounter with universal, divine will, it happened after I had given myself the extraordinary luxury of allowing myself to look at my own sense of deficiency for a considerable period of time – as much as a half hour. That's a long time to concentrate on something I don't like about myself. I investigated how my sense of deficiency showed up, and itemized my usual attempts at compensation. After I had examined my issue with will over and over, I came into the spontaneous presence of the platinum bar replacing my spine. A feeling of contentment and not having to necessarily *do something* arrived, as well as a sense that will was more available to me than I had thought. Only later did I learn that platinum is the color and element that describes the essential aspect that corresponds to the words "universal will." I had come into the presence, in my body, of an essential aspect.

We have already seen several conditions of the thirty-five divine body-forms:

- ❧ Each is associated with a particular noun of value

- ❧ Each is unique

- ❧ Each has an opposite that is also unique but is not an essential aspect

- ❧ Each has its unique color

- ❧ Each is a quality of the divine

Now we have added two more conditions:

- ❧ Each has a false, shadow version of itself

- ❧ All of the essential aspects are discoverable in every human being; they're just hidden

There's more. The essential aspects can be appreciated as a color and also by texture, taste, smell, sound, viscosity, luminosity, density, and affect. We've seen some of these dimensions in our examples of body-forms. More exposure to the essential aspects tends to increase a person's sensitivity to all the dimensions. But everybody's different. One dimension may be so subtle for you that it doesn't seem to manifest. I have good hearing and a lot of interest in music, but I don't *hear* the essential aspects, and I seldom taste or smell them. Like a lot of people I've worked with, I can readily see their color, feel their density and viscosity, and note their luminosity and texture, and that's enough to evoke them.

Some essential aspects correspond to an earthly element, a gem, or a fruit. For those body-forms that are represented on the periodic table, the dimensions of color, luminosity, viscosity, and density track 1:1 with their natural-world elements.

Strength is a ruby, and *compassion* is an emerald. *Will* is white in color and substance, *universal will* is platinum in color and substance, and *existence* is molybdenum, No. 42 on the periodic table. *Truth* is gold. All of these aspects have appeared these ways in my own torso. *Passionate love* is pomegranate.

The thirty-five divine body-forms have a purity that feels spontaneous. They have a simple directness and perfection that allow them to be appreciated and understood without words. They feel pleasurable, but not as if they're fulfilling a need. For us modern people, pleasure seems conditional. In the non-stop pursuit of comfort and ease, we end up defeating our own pursuit by spending so much time on it. We invoke our own disappointment. Many of us are self-frustrating machines. The invocation of the essential aspects isn't like that.

Mostly they're released not by avoiding our suffering, but by diving straight into it. By accepting the truth of our suffering, we discover a way out. This is a therapy for modern people. Anyone can benefit. At the very least, you'll get respite for a while, and when coupled with a coherent path that includes work on relaxing built-up identities, their appearance can help on the way to a deeper, more satisfying way of life.

Chapter 18

Can This Be True?

All of this is more than a little strange. How am I supposed to believe any of this exists in a world of natural laws, including physics, chemistry, and medicine?

I don't think the body-form method interacts with physical laws. It doesn't need to. I'm a rationalist when it comes to the everyday, cellular world. I read *Scientific American* for fun. I believe that an MD has the expertise to keep my body healthy. The laws of physics, from Newton through Einstein and beyond, hold true all the time for the bodies, forces, and waves that they describe. I don't happen to believe in mind over matter, but if you do, that's fine. As far as I can tell, none of the typically described paranormal conditions overlap with the body-form experiences. You can believe in the supernatural or not, and the body-form experience will be the same.

Whatever the body-form experiences are, they exist in a protected realm of their own. They don't interfere with my physical body, and they don't transition me to a non-physical universe. They don't endanger my normal conditions. Their realm probably is lodged in my imagination, and probably is driven by the same forces that everyday consciousness is. No one can be sure of this without knowing more about consciousness than neurology and other sciences have come up with so far.

Body-form experiences do not disrupt the rules, conditions and laws of everyday life. They form a small, additive room in my life. This odd little realm has its own conditions and rules, that's true. But they're not particularly out of harmony with the usual conditions and rules.

So I'm happy to call this a realm of the imagination, with a couple of caveats. It feels more real than that. You'll probably experience that. It doesn't feel like I'm making things up as I let my interior show me things. And the realm of body-forms also has a narrowly defined vocabulary of colors, symbols and experiences that seem to be universal – the same color means the same thing for me or you, for instance – and that seem to be useful to my human condition. This is the kind of new reality that Freud presumably bumped up against when he discovered the id and the superego. Those too were non-cellular forces or structures found throughout humanity, with universal meanings and principles.

If you want to call a body-form exercise a mystical experience you can, but you don't have to. Many of my clients just shrug and say body-forms are what happen when they "go inside" in a particular way. First an object

that represents your concern – your suffering *du jour* –
arises, and after looking at it a while, it disappears. Then a
period of well-being sets in, and sometimes after that a
new object appears that is extremely cool and beautiful,
and takes you on a short trip outside your normal
boundaries. All of this happens in a temporarily carved-out
section of the body, with the rest of the body looking
normal. No one does anything to carve out the body-form
section. It just happens. The curtains part, the show goes
on, and then the curtains close and the regular old organs
return to their rightful spots.

After a body-form exercise I don't have to commit to a
new way of acting, a new way of being, a new set of ethics
or laws, new precepts or new beliefs. I don't even need to
interpret what happened briefly inside me.

I just let the body-form experience happen, and if it
seems appropriate, do it again in a week or two. I might feel
better at the end, but I don't feel like a different person or
like anything particularly remarkable happened to me. I
wasn't hypnotized, and I wasn't force-fed an experience. It
was my experience, directed by me if by anyone.

So what's the point of it all? Body-form experiences
seem to be a built-in hedge against suffering, an antidote to
the voice in my head telling me that I should avoid looking
too long at negative emotions. The first body-form
represents an emotional suffering of mine. As a reward for
spending time with it instead of avoiding it, the second
body-form appears, representing the inner strength – my
inborn support system – that can over time negate that
form of emotional suffering.

Beyond that, some clients discover that body-forms
are a more accurate representation of who they are than
the self-images that they produce when trying to please
others. Maybe I really am made of space, light, and divine

qualities. Maybe I'm born with all the value that I'll ever need. I still need to operate within the conditions of the everyday society, but I can feel wholehearted and free inside.

Chapter 19

Getting to Know Me

Before you encounter a divine object such as a red brick of strength or a feeling of the torso saturating itself in yellow, you'll probably spend a while in the presence of a muddier, duller and less pleasant object. We've discussed this in relation to the divine objects, but it would be a mistake to see the first object simply as a barrier that needs to be broken through. While life seems to have means to ends, in another way anything I call a "means" is also an end in itself. Studying my own suffering is enough sometimes to end my suffering, at least temporarily. We complain to rid ourselves of the complaint.

For most people, the entry point to a body-form experience is through a troubling emotion. You felt ignored by your partner this morning, and you're carrying some residual anger. Your boss is demeaning. You don't have enough friends. Your children are disrespectful. You can't stand your job. You've been depressed for the past week. It might be big or small. But in one way or another, things are going wrong and you're suffering.

I ask my client to shut her eyes and scan her torso, neck and head for a localized feeling that isn't gastrointestinal. It can be a feeling of tension, heat, cold, energy, or something else. After ten to thirty seconds, typically, she tells me what she has found.

The most common first objects include:

- ֍ a tense sphere in the solar plexus

- ֍ a flat, thin, curving band that spans the forehead, just under the skin

- ֍ a V-shaped wedge inside the jawline from ear to ear

- ֍ a short cylinder stuck in the front of the throat

- ֍ a dowel or shield running across the top of the shoulders

- ֍ a rectangular object in the front third of the chest

These are just the most common ones. Many other shapes appear, in any part of the torso, neck or head.

The first object typically is made of rubber or lead or aluminum or rock. It can also be empty or gaseous or liquid. It is usually gray, brown, black, or tan. If it starts out another, brighter color, it will often fade to tan or gray as it is observed. It may be attached to a part of the body, but usually it is floating. The internal organs that would normally fill its space will clear out temporarily and leave a two- or three-inch empty space all around the body-form object, which might be an inch wide or a foot or more wide. At first the object is usually still, but as more attention is paid, it may pulse or move to a new spot for a minute or two before resting again.

When I ask for its dimensions, they don't necessarily conform to what's possible in physical anatomy. For instance, the client might find a cylinder that is ten inches in diameter and two inches high sitting in the middle of her neck. Her physical neck is only six inches in diameter.

The client may look at the object from all sides, may enter it and look at it from the inside, or may even become a little person sitting on it or diving into it. The object usually remains inside, where it was first found, but may also project itself outside the body for a while.

It will start to move or change after being observed for a while. The shift may start after as little as two minutes, or it can take upwards of an hour before it changes. The median is ten minutes. There's no telling in advance. Presumably it takes longer for a more pronounced emotional issue, less time for a more trivial trouble.

When it does move or change, most often it will shrink slowly, often fading in color as it reduces. Sometimes it will shrink until it disappears. More often it will shrink to a size less than a quarter, and then either break up and dissipate into its surroundings or move out. If it moves out, it sometimes just pokes its way out the skin, or it will slide into the throat and out the mouth, or it may lose structure, liquify, and pool in the bottom of the stomach before draining out the perineum. Less often it may leave out through the eye sockets or open a hole in the crown and push through the top of the head.

Sometimes it will leave fragments behind. If the client keeps attention on the fragments, they will either disappear or coalesce into another emotionally based object, and the whole process starts over again. The replacement object usually shrinks and disappears much faster. Rarely, it will again fragment and reconstitute for a third take.

Once the first object or its replacement has fully disappeared, the client's impulse is to end the experience by opening her eyes. I instruct the client to continue concentrating on where the object used to be, which is now an empty space. If the object has left an impression of itself behind, the faint form will disappear in less than a minute. The cocoon that was carved out for the object will remain, though. The empty hollow may be black, or it may have a color associated with it.

My notion, although I can't prove it in any way, is that the object disappears when it has been thoroughly seen for what it is. The object represents an emotional issue that normally is avoided or rejected for its suffering effect, with little attention paid to its whole self. I don't like being demeaned by my boss, and feel prickly and hot and angry when it happens. But I'm not really thinking about what it is about being demeaned that is unpleasant. I don't say to myself, "Hmm, what is it to be demeaned? Where have I encountered this before? Does it remind me of my father? Why do I feel that I have to defend myself from this feeling? How does feeling demeaned get in the way of my relationship with my boss?" I just do what I need to get rid of the feeling. Given a chance, I might find "being demeaned" to be a whole course of study. But most of the time, I just want to stop the bleeding, lick my wounds, and get on with life.

Maybe, though, during a body-form session, the mechanics of feeling demeaned are opened up to me. Maybe in some way, the feeling and effect of being demeaned gets seen thoroughly for what it is, a kind of drab defensiveness that crowds out my supportive, resilient core. And maybe the body-form looks at itself as a

teacher, showing me what "being demeaned" looks like
without the prickly emotional feelings that usually take the
place of an objective review. I like to think that when the
first body-form feels that it has been seen for what it is,
rather than hated and pushed away, it says, "Thank you,"
and waves goodbye as it disappears.

At this point, the first body-form having completely
vanished, I ask my client, "How do you feel?"

The answer is usually: "I feel good." Often there's
another sentence added, to the effect of, "It's like I feel
good all over."

One of the more peculiar traits of this peculiar
business is that spending time with a single emotional
issue – symbolized by the first object that appears – is
enough to clear out, for a time, *all* of your emotional issues.
The sense of well-being after the disappearance of, say, a
gray sphere in the solar plexus, is big and full and
thorough.

This feeling of well-being typically continues for
several minutes. It can continue into the day, too.

After getting used to the experience, by the third or
fourth session the client will start to have new experiences
that follow the feeling of respite. If they keep their eyes
closed long enough and concentrate on the emptiness
within while the feeling of well-being saturates them, a new
body-form will show up. This one is *always* a divine object.
Its color is bright, it lacks tension, and it expands as it is
viewed. The feelings that accompany this body-form may
include awe, sweetness, contentment, and its own specific
delights – effervescence if it's yellow, full-bloodedness if
red, peace if black.

Simply put, the client concentrates on his own
suffering, allows it to show itself fully, and is rewarded with
its absence during a short period akin to grace. When the

grace ends, if the client is observant, a second reward arises: a view of the inborn, divine support for that psychological issue, and a glimpse of the heaven within.

In a way, this is a theatrical, symbolic miniaturization of the dark night of the soul. Whether depicted by St. John of the Cross or a drunkologue at an Alcoholics Anonymous meeting, a dark night of the soul goes like this: A deep suffering consumes a man (or woman). He can't seem to do anything about it. He sinks farther and farther into it. It blinds him to the rest of the world. He reaches the bottom, where he encounters both helplessness and hopelessness. No help. No hope. Both have to be present. The future becomes empty and unimaginable. Grace steps in. The divine opens up. A way out, through a previously unknown inner or outer strength, appears.

In the body-form experience, a simple suffering appears. You examine it without a sense of needing to fix it or avoid it. This corresponds to the dark night's understanding that you don't have or need hope or help. You surrender to the body-form, turn it over and stare at it, and recognize that you don't have any power over it. It's just there, a dull, muddy object in your torso or neck or head. Once you've accepted it and accepted that you don't need power over it, grace enters. The body-form disappears, leaving a quiet, lovely emptiness. And the divine has room or reason to enter.

Chapter 20

Prep Work

So far, the body-form method I have described seems to work randomly. Close your eyes and see what shows up. An emotional issue will express itself in the first body-form. I won't know what the body-form represents, and I may get through the entire experience without using familiar psychological concepts to describe what I have been investigating. In at least half of my sessions, neither the client nor I identify afterward what issue the first body-form represented. The salutary effects don't require post-mortem discrimination.

But what if you want to address a specific issue? What if you worry that you have a bad temper and want to do something about it, now, finally? What if you can't watch the news without feeling terrified, and you notice that others shrug at the world's misfortunes? What if your life is vaguely unfulfilling, and you can't figure out why?

First of all, notice that your issues are the same as everyone else's. You've exaggerated one set of deficiencies, while your neighbor has exaggerated another set. But you have your neighbor's worries, and your neighbor has yours. There's a finite set of issues, once they're boiled down, and an even smaller set of defenses that you can raise to keep them at bay.

The point isn't that misery loves company. It's that there's hope. If your issues aren't unique, then experts are out there, and you might stumble into a treatment that works for you. With this in mind, you might have tried out a therapist or a self-help book or two. In the body-form method, your inner work can lead you to an experience of one or more of thirty-five properties of the divine, each of which provides a support for a specific constellation of common emotional issues. *Strength*, for instance, which appears as a red full-bloodedness, typically appears at the end of a session in which a client was exploring their feelings of being stupid or weak. If your concern is your own procrastination, the session may land in an inner field of white, the body-form representation of divine *will*.

The body-form method can be tailored to address what you want to work on now, today. It can also be adapted to diagnose and set your priorities for future sessions.

One way is simple. Before going inside and asking the size, shape, density, color questions, the interviewer can ask the client to focus for a moment on something that has been bugging them recently.

"Bring to mind an emotional issue that arose earlier today," I say to the client. "Don't tell me what it is. Just nod when you've got an issue in mind. Okay. You've got one, I see. Now let it go, close your eyes, and search for something in your torso, neck or head ..." And away we go.

Often enough, but not always, the first body-form that appears represents the last emotional issue in mind. One advantage for a newbie to the body-form method is that the morning's emotional issue probably isn't huge. It's more likely that the first body-form will need only a few minutes to be seen and disappear, rather than an hour or more. The newbie can see quick results, which helps people continue on a repetitive program. Like most other teachings, this one requires a fair number of repetitions – lots of sessions – for its benefits to unfold fully.

Another way to direct the experience is to spend a quarter-hour to a half-hour exploring your ideas about your issue, before going inside. Stay in your head and talk to your interviewer about your history with the issue, your beliefs about how the issue cripples you, your dislike of the people or circumstances that trigger the issue, and, especially, just when in your childhood you first noticed the issue. Engage in a little talk therapy. Get the issue out front and in the atmosphere. Then start the body-form, with the interviewer as usual saying, "Close your eyes, and search for something in your torso, neck or head ..."

A third, highly structured way, is to map your issues and pursue them one by one, working through each one until the divine aspect that supports you in it appears. Sometimes I take my clients through a short curriculum, offering them a series of sequential sessions. The first might lead to the body-form of *curiosity*, the second to *strength*, the third to *will*, etcetera. In this practice, the work isn't personalized to the issues that dominate the client's sense of self, but mechanically works through the full range of issues and their supportive body-forms. This is tricky, nuanced, and requires some mastery.

While the set of thirty-five divine body-forms are properties of God or consciousness or a hidden reality, they are related to specifically human concerns, especially feelings of dissatisfaction or deficiency. They seem to be sorted and ready to address human hardship. As such, they are particularly prominent in the front-end of a spiritual journey, which often revolves around ways to dissociate from burdensome emotions. The body-forms help people deprogram their inner critic's running narrative. When they are accessed, the divine body-forms tend to show up in correspondence to what you need right now. If you're feeling weak, *strength* will show up. If you're feeling lazy, *will* shows up. If you're feeling overwhelmed, *power* might show up. They're not just a comfort but an inner reservoir of support. They're always available, it turns out. The hard part is deciding to access them, taking that deep breath, plugging your nose, and saying, "OK. Let's see who I am right now."

Chapter 21

❧❧

Variations on a Theme

While the first object is usually well defined and is clearly an object lodged in a part of your body, the second, divine, body-form may appear in other ways than as a manipulable solid object.

A client might encounter a ray of bright sunshine, or a distant bright white sky. In either case, its whiteness is blinding at its faraway source, and as the ray approaches it is tinged with yellow like a regular sunbeam. As you'll remember, this experience represents the concept of *trust*. Or the client will find her torso opening up into a wide space that extends out as if infinite, and may include galaxies and a sense of space flight. This might not simply be the black of *power* or stillness, but, like the sunbeam, might represent a safety net for the repositioning of your entire worldview. The galaxies indicate different realms and dimensions with different conditions. The space is your freedom to go where you want and visit whichever galaxy you want, with no limits. Most of us are wary of breaking the boundaries of our beliefs; this spacious freedom reminds us that chaos is a fiction and that our imagination is allowed to roam free, and will always encounter an organizing principle. When we break down boundaries we meet a different world, but it's organized and complete in itself.

Sometimes the divine body-form colors will arise during the session's encounter with the first body-form. A rock in the pit of the stomach may first appear to be green or red. If it's green, then you probably are exploring something that you feel ashamed about, and you need a little self-*compassion* to get started. If it's red, you're probably exploring something that feels dangerous, and you need *strength* to see you through the process. The green or red will fade after a minute or so, and the rock will turn the usual gray or brown or black or tan before it disappears.

Often, the client will encounter more than one color at a time. A blue gem may be surrounded by a pink glow, for instance. Perhaps it's the blue gem of *knowingness*, in a field of pink *personal love*. Maybe the client is seeing the circumstances in which wisdom and childlike love can amplify each other.

The Pearl often appears, directly or indirectly. The Pearl, you'll recall, is our recognition of our personal essence. It's the full container of our soul. It gives us a sense of a particular self that doesn't need fixed roles or identities. Instead, the Pearl can take on whatever temporary role or set of beliefs is needed to get through the current moment. It's a kind of chameleon. When encountered as itself, it is an actual pearl, or a milky white sphere of any size. It has a distinct feeling of being light and airy but not diffuse. It is consistent and rich. This is the experience my now-wife had on our first meeting. Usually the Pearl expands to fill the torso to the skin, and can also expand well outside the confines of the body. And it can change color. It might appear that your entire torso has turned red. You have the same consistent airiness of the Pearl experience, but you're red. You are in the *red pearl*; you are your own essence of *strength*, through and through. The pearl can appear as the medium of personalness for any of the other thirty-four divine body-forms.

Another embracing experience that might happen at the start or the end of a session is to find sheets or banners of purple, especially in the cranium. I can't find any documentation on this one, so I have to guess: Purple in many traditions represents royalty, as in kings, queens, princes and princesses. That's the common cultural symbolism. The purple found inside may raise esteem, allowing the client to overcome a feeling that he or she isn't worthy of a divine experience. The client is her own princess, deserving of the body-form experiences. Some clients seem to find it useful to bring the purple in sight through many sessions. Curiously, it seldom appears alone. Another color or object will usually accompany it.

Finally, the end of the divine body-form experience is usually abrupt. The body-form will simply disappear, and the client's eyes will open. The median length of a divine body-form experience is five minutes, much shorter than the time typically spent with the first body-form.

Shapes of Truth

Chapter 22

Stories

Eyes closed and resting after the disappearance of a first body-object, Angie discovered a beach in her midsection, at the edge of a dark, calm sea. She floated in the blue sky, as if suspended by an antigravity force, looking down at the seascape, feeling a warm sun on her back. After a while she decided to take a swim, and the next thing she knew, she was frolicking with green mermaids and mermen around the ocean bottom, and pausing as gorgeous yellow tropical fish flashed by, winking and waving at her with friendly smiles. All of this happened inside her torso.

Before going into the experience, Angie had been complaining of loneliness and how she missed having a partner or at least good friends around. She felt isolated and discouraged. She was OK being introverted, but this was different.

The key word here was "loneliness." She didn't mind being alone. She minded being lonely. Loneliness always traces to feeling unloved. And feeling unloved always traces to a vague fear that you are unlovable. This is a common feeling, shared by just about everyone at some time.

A dark sea is foreboding. What is hidden underneath? Diving into a dark sea alone raises the prospect of drowning. Before diving in, Angie floats in a blue sky of knowledge, and feels sunbeams on her back – *trust* that this hidden world is safe to explore. She takes the plunge, and discovers that she can stay alive without breathing, in this watery realm. Nothing around her is harming her. It's safe. And even better, the little fish notice her, welcome her, and presumably love her.

A complex body-form experience can develop a linear story-line. The colors of the elements of the story often correspond in meaning to the divine body-form colors. A blue sky reminds Angie of spacious *knowingness* that expands into wisdom. Green mermaids and mermen provide the comfort of *compassion*; they too know the ways of suffering, and the beauty of being relieved of emotional concern. They are loving. Yellow fish are open, joyful and *curious*. And oddly, she is in a medium of *water*, which represents the very state of being human. So the story might be telling her that she can be loved, curious, wise, and safe in a sense of her own humanity that operates differently, that allows her to breathe underwater. Metaphorically, that is. And foremost, she is loved.

At first, these stories seem to be a clue to who we *can* be. Only after a number of repetitions and visits does it begin to dawn on the client that she actually *is* the divine body-forms, that every time she peels away a layer of defense, she will come upon the light of *trust*, the blue skies of *knowingness*, the green skins of *compassion*, and the yellow smiles of open *curiosity*.

It's worth noting that sometimes pretty stories arise before the first body-form – the one representing the client's everyday suffering – has completely disappeared. This corresponds to the notion that you can replace a bad feeling or habit with a good feeling or habit, by will. People are fond of saying, "Think positive." But that doesn't work here. If you find yourself drawn to a rosy picture off to the side of a gray blob, return to the gray blob. Ignore the rosy picture. It's probably an attempt by your inner critic – what psychologists call the superego – to take back control and keep you from discovering the true flimsiness of your collected emotional burdens. Return your attention to the gray blob until it disappears. Only then will you feel the empty sense of well-being that might lead you to a divine body-form experience in its full splendor.

Some linear stories provide respite from fears. Others provide clues to freedom from fear. This isn't the same as dream interpretation, and it's not Jungian archetype storytelling. Dream interpretation is a form of free association that can lead the mind to discovering what it is afraid of. A divine body-form experience doesn't explain anything; it just shows you who you really are. Jungian archetypes are artifacts of the cultural norms; they separate your world into right and wrong, or good and bad. They help you rank yourself, compare yourself to others, and see what is expected of you in society. They belong in the world of ethics.

The divine body-forms are not ethical or moral. They represent who you are by nature, before you've been taught right versus wrong and good versus bad. The odd thing is that every one of the thirty-five accessible divine body-forms is found on the right side of right vs. wrong, and the good side of good versus bad.

We're rigged to the good.

We are so good that we don't have to learn how to be good. What three-year-old won't give away his peanut butter sandwich a few times before realizing that he's left without a sandwich? Only later are we told how to differentiate good from bad, first vaguely, and after five years old, rigorously. We are introduced to "bad" and "wrong" as new, defining characteristics. In a way, the divine body-forms bring the adult back to his or her true nature as it exhibited itself in early childhood. You knew yourself, back then, as boundless *curiosity*, boundless *strength*, boundless *will*, boundless *compassion*, and boundless *power*. But as you were taught to conform, to follow the adult rules, you lost touch with your boundless core qualities and built up thick layers of civilized distrust.

One more word about story-telling and divine body-form experiences: Once in a while you might be taken into a rich, complex story that operates differently.

Some years ago I had been studying *will* as a divine body-form during a meditation, when suddenly I saw a vision of the Hindu lord Krishna sitting gleefully atop the earth, which was on fire underneath him, and slowly burning away its familiar colors from top to bottom, the green and blue turning a charred black while flames roared and licked at Krishna's legs. On either side of Krishna, crumbling neon billboards flickered with messages. On the left, the message was "Delusions." On the right, the message was "Grandeur." Behind the tableau, a giant Our Lady of Guadalupe stood still and strong, her usual golden rays transformed into a wide horseshoe of molten gold that circulated and glowed in a self-replenishing stream around her.

The message to me afterward was clear: You're going to disrupt your narcissism (the delusions of grandeur) and burn down your entire world, in a holy fire, but the *truth* (the circulating, molten gold) will protect you, along with Our Lady of Guadalupe (who, by the way, is known to Biblical scholars to be partially representative of Revelations' Queen of the Apocalypse). I wasn't just burning down my world, but the whole world.

This vision was a handy support for me as I moved into the crushing, fiery, difficult work of ego death, which happened to be where I was in my spiritual path at the time. This vision and others like it showed me what I had to do, and reminded me of the reward at the end, which was the laughing Krishna supervising the whole mishmash. It made it a little easier to go on with the work. As it turned out, studying ego death for me was a period of investigating my story lines of trauma, achievement, and success and failure. I investigated my stories – the claims that I was a thread of connected experiences, tracing an arc of meaning – and eventually recognized that none of the individual stories was particularly helpful for me to accurately assess where I was right then. If I didn't need the stories, maybe I wasn't the stories. This stage of my ego death ended with the conclusive statement, "I don't believe my stories."

Shapes of Truth

Chapter 23

Blue Boy

y 2010 or so, accessing body-forms had become a pillar of my self-inquiry. I was immersed in the Ridhwan School, but I had many of my bigger revelations in the office of octogenarian Bob Birnbaum, a fellow Ridhwan student who had been my therapist since my marriage dissolved in 2006.

For a year or so, one particular body-form would return once or twice a month in my sessions with Bob. This was not one of the thirty-five divine body-forms. It wasn't that simple or direct. It was a complex object, about two feet high, lodged in my central torso, and wore a tent-like smock that covered it from neck to toes. The smock was blue gray. Above the smock emerged the head of a seven-year-old boy with a washed-out, blank expression, and rising from his hair was an ordinary candle, lit with a steady yellow flame.

Blue Boy was me.

This was the embodiment of my memory of my childhood. It was more specifically the memory of the child who lived in reaction to my mother's schizoaffective disorder. Her illness usually looked like depression, but was punctuated by occasional, short psychotic breaks, frequent bursts of rage, sudden mood changes, and substantial periods of relative normality and lucidity. When her symptoms were active, it was not a happy home.

Blue Boy was a particularly stubborn set of ego obstacles. He was like a package of preliminary body-forms, wrapped up in an entire self. Usually the first body-form represents only a small piece of the manifold of ego obstacles I've built up over the years – just one of as many as thirty-five categories of psychodynamic conflict. Blue Boy might have had all thirty-five going at once, or at least three or four. I can't remember now.

When I evaluated my childhood dealings with my mother, Blue Boy would appear. Sometimes it was in Bob's office, and other times at home or in the car as I thought about what I was learning about my mother and my childhood. Much of my work with Bob was ordinary psychotherapy. But Blue Boy took on a life of his own, carrying me with him. Blue Boy represented the me who had been entangled with my mother's problems. And he was more than that. Because my inner critic had saturated me with Blue Boy's story and ensuing rule, my mother's lesson that others should always be held higher than me, were all that mattered, I assumed that Blue Boy was an accurate and complete symbolic representation of myself at seven years old. In a way, I assumed that Blue Boy was what the books call the "inner child," representing something inescapable about my past.

I gave Blue Boy my full attention. He showed no expression, but the affect I noticed while contemplating him was sadness. He wasn't allowed to be exuberantly happy, because there were starving children in Asia. Whose words might those have been? I learned a lot about compassion by spending quiet time with Blue Boy. He helped me love myself deeply for the first time: I loved him, and he was the me that I believed had engendered my present self. Our encounters – my adult self looking down toward my belly and seeing him standing in there, downcast and alone – were sad and sweet. He never changed. He would have dissolved into a puddle of pathos if it hadn't been for the little flame sticking out of his head. The candle seemed like his preservation of hope for something better, and while I certainly had borrowed the image from Dickens' *Christmas Carol*, it also resonated with the flame of enlightenment that erupts from the Buddha's head.

For a long time – a year or more – it didn't occur to me to question Blue Boy's reality. But around the time I started to seriously question the idea that I was still the product of my mom's problems, Blue Boy began to feel dull. I particularly noticed how Blue Boy had no dynamism.

One afternoon a Polaroid print suddenly appeared in front of Blue Boy, again inside my torso, a blurry shot of a different me caught exuberantly mid-leap between stones in the neighborhood creek, playing with a friend. I noticed how much more dynamic the Polaroid was, even though it was two-dimensional and Blue Boy presumably stood in three dimensions. I puzzled over that as I looked in on the two boys every few days. I recognized that exuberant boy had lived just as many years as Blue Boy. And then on one visit a new thought popped up: "Childhood wasn't sad. It wasn't always exuberant, either. If it was difficult, the right word is 'confusing.'"

The tonality of my childhood memories shifted, some of them quite abruptly. What had been scary scenes of my mother in a psychotic break became pictures of a child looking on in puzzlement as his mother inaccurately viewed the world. Resentments toward parental behaviors that seemed to have crippled me turned into fascination that the same memories were now object lessons that could lead me to understanding and lightness. Raising these memories, seeing how distorted they were, paying close attention to the shadowy nature of the patterns sketched on my wall, in my torso became the very engine of my movement out of a dank cave and into the daylight.

Later I discovered that the memories weren't so much distorted as they were incomplete. It's an important distinction to point out here, because the question rises of how the body, which is an accurate truth-teller, can allow a seemingly false picture of me – Blue Boy – to arise as an embodied object.

It turns out that objects like Blue Boy (and exuberant boy, too) are not truthful in their content as preserved things of the past. It is probably impossible to accurately preserve things from the past. Body-forms like Blue Boy are a truthful depiction of what my inner critic is telling me to believe. They are a truthful depiction of the experience I am having at the time.

Once I recognized that Blue Boy wasn't my only childhood self, and that all of my memories of childhood self were two-dimensional, and that confusion was a better description than sadness or suffering for the difficulties of growing up, Blue Boy stopped appearing.

Remember the grayish-brown liquid stain that Annie describes in the book's Foreword, which is replaced by her *pearl*? That first, often ugly body-form is an accurate, unadorned representation of a form of suffering. It's not a facet of God. It's not one of the thirty-five divine body-forms. In my own experience it usually represents a concept that, when described by words in my mind, is torturing me under the guidance of the nagging voice in my head. It's me feeling bad for something I did, or worried that I will soon fail in some way. The seeming purpose of its rising in my body is to give me the opportunity to stay concentrated on it long enough to see it completely. And when I have, it disappears and takes its suffering with it, at least for a little while. This is where we get the common expression, "I've seen through that." Seeing *through* something means giving it the opportunity for its falseness to depart by seeing the falseness clearly and accurately – truthfully – as itself. Once Blue Boy's rigid, thin claim of sadness and pathos was allowed to appear fully, Blue Boy departed.

Another way of saying this is that the body allows an emotional wound to be opened and kept open until its discharges no longer cause revulsion, fainting, and avoidance. Instead, the wound is examined freely by the person who feels wounded. And then the wound closes all on its own. A bath of tears can do the same thing.

Likewise, a divine body-form rises to be seen, and once its lesson is taught it changes form. It is seldom afterward seen as a distinct object, and instead is integrated in a way that allows it to retain a more subtle influence on me. Often what happens is that as the essential aspect is integrated, I lose my capacity to retrieve its gross structure while I retain its ability to express its color. So I no longer notice a platinum bar going up my spine, but occasionally when I come into contact with a need for *universal will*, I'll notice my body disappearing into the color of platinum. And once I've been fully reminded of the dynamic and active presence of universal will, the color will disappear and the next moment will arise. And the color may arise again when I need it again.

We've seen a recurring theme that the body-forms are involved in accuracy, truthfulness, objectivity, and erosion of distortion. Truth-seeking is not just a hallmark of the path of spirituality; it may be its only activity. Beyond the psychological context we've been exploring, body-forms may have a human purpose related to our understanding and use of truth itself.

If not for the body-forms, I might never have relinquished Blue Boy's grip on my belief in myself, and might not have found the path to live as a free adult, unfettered by the confusion of childhood.

More than that, with time I've come to know that the thirty-five are always in me, acting on me, moving through me, subtly and without a need for display. The body-forms accompany me at all times. They allow me to appreciate people and things accurately, and together they provide most of my tools for joining in with the world's self-evident, intimate, omnipresent, and precious capacities for love and awe.

Chapter 24

✒ ✑

A (Very) Little
Chomsky

efore he was a leftist social and political observer,
Noam Chomsky made a spectacular discovery as a
young professor at MIT. Studying language
structures, he noticed that they all seemed to
share some illogical peculiarities. He eventually proved
that language is its own faculty in the brain, and that
humans are forced into a specific and peculiar syntax. It
isn't the only syntax possible, but it's the only one we all
share. The result of this theory of "universal grammar" is
that we seem to be born with our language syntax. The
hidden structure of language is inborn, not taught.

Chomsky first published his discovery in 1957. He has
written books about it and continues to expand on the
discovery in papers to this day. At the end of each paper or
book he cautions that all he has proven is that syntax is
inborn. He remains as troubled now as he was in 1957 that
an inborn syntax is insufficient to support a system of

semantics, or meaning. A syntactical structure doesn't provide a specific route to meaning. Chomsky hasn't proven an inborn system of meaning.

What if in addition to an inborn syntax, I was born with an interior set of thirty-five body-forms? Would they operate as a proto-vocabulary? And if I had a rudimentary vocabulary to add to an inborn syntax, would that take me all the way to meaning?

And where would that put morality? Is it learned as a religious or political ethical code, or do I have an inborn vocabulary that naturally rigs me toward *right* or *good*? If I find it, maybe I can stop listening to the preacher and instead go inside to find the truth. Maybe it's already stored inside me. Maybe it is me.

Chapter 25

&❧&

There You Have It

Garren's mistakes plagued him. A talented, well-paid software programmer, his perfectionism seemed to cut him off from feeling satisfaction at work.

"I know I'm the best programmer on the floor," he said at the beginning of a session with me, "but I always think I'm one mistake away from being fired."

When I suggested that he feel into his torso, the first object Garren encountered was a dull, hard, black stone caught in his ribs. After a while it moved up into his skull, where it morphed into a metal band around his cranium that pressed painfully against his forehead.

"This is giving me a headache," he said.

"You mean that literally?" I asked.

"Yes, I've got a mild headache all of a sudden."

"So you have a metal band pressing against your forehead, and you also have a mild headache now, right?"

"Right."

"Can you tolerate it?" I asked.

"Sure."

I waited.

"Oh," he said.

I waited.

"Oh?" I finally asked. "What just happened?"

"The band relaxed," Garren said, "and then it kind of floated away. But that's not all. When it released itself, my whole head opened up, and now it's like it's part of the sky. It's just blue sky. It's like there's no top to my head."

I waited.

"How does that feel?" I asked.

"It feels good. No, it's more like, I feel good. All over. How funny. It feels really good."

Now see for yourself. You might notice some common reflections as you engage with your own experience of divine body-forms. The episodic feeling of well-being, of respite from the usual emotional concerns, can become a familiar destination after a number of body-form experience repetitions. This sense of well-being is akin, I think, to the Buddhist notion of equanimity. In this sensed state, the same world surrounds me as before. It is dynamic, full of things and people, triggers and reactions, highs and lows. The only thing is, that's all outside. Inside I'm peaceful and non-reactive, neither high nor low. Yes, the people and things are engaged in their usual interactions outside. But instead of triggering a reaction, they're just kind of fascinating. They don't present themselves as threats and desires, or in urgent need of correction or attachment. They're just there, and I'm here, and all's well in the world. If I'm not trying to be somewhere else, I tend to slow down and appreciate where I am, which simply means that I'm noticing more of my proximate surroundings. I feel like an objective observer, or a loving participant. I feel content as is. That's equanimity in a nutshell.

If I experience that enough times and take special notice of my ability to live fruitfully within equanimity's strange new conditions, I might start playing with the possibility of living in equanimity even when I'm not in a body-form experience. I might start asking myself, what is dissatisfaction, anyway, if it is so unnecessary? If I can sit within one formerly dissatisfying experience in a new equanimity, can I sit within another? The body-form experience becomes a finger pointing to a new truth, but a difficult one, that may require lots of investigation before my prior assumptions can get out of the way.

And what then is a particular body-form to me? Of course it's interesting if I'm Garren and my head has fallen off to be replaced by a blue sky. But why no head? Why blue? Maybe there's something to explore in these metaphoric experiences that feel so real. Maybe the metaphors are there to help me understand myself better. Could I become my own dream interpreter, tarot card reader, astrologer, tea-leaf reader, prompting my mind to harness its power of free association into a specific room of my psyche? What if I have thirty-five rooms, each full of its own cobwebs, waiting to be observed, cleaned and refreshed? Maybe each room has its own color and symbol, so I know where I am. Maybe my headless room is the one where my ego needs to be cleaned out. Maybe my blue room is the one where my know-it-allness needs to be cleaned out. Maybe if I clean up enough rooms I'll start to feel like the lord of my own house. If that happened, then my collection of body-form experiences might start to feel like soul work, as if I've accidentally begun to cleanse my soul of its distortions. And maybe, over time, in some ways,

I could feel refined and purified, or even simplified, down to my singular, intimate, and limitless essence.

Chapter 26

❧❧

Catalog
Of Body-Forms

The final section of the book lists the thirty-five
divine body-forms, as discovered and catalogued
by Hameed Ali. Everything descriptive in this
chapter has been confirmed by Ali through
observations of classes and individual sessions with friends
and Diamond Approach followers. I boiled down his
writings about them into a page for each, which he
reviewed and edited for accuracy.

These are probably our first and original inherent
vocabulary of manifest forms and of concepts. They might
be seen as the faces of God, or the highest level of Platonic
ideals, or our inborn moral compass and decision-making
reference.

The first five I've listed were known to the Sufi, and I
refer to them as the big five, because they are jacks-of-all-
trades and can be useful in many if not most of the
common human experiences, dissatisfactions, and

difficulties. Next are four aspects that are particularly prominent in Ali's teaching. The rest of the aspects are presented in no particular order, although I've bunched the love aspects together.

It is striking that there are so few. Ali has gone out of his way for many years to discover the aspects, and these probably represent most if not all of the inborn human vocabulary of manifest forms. (He mentions that he has run across two more – one represents something he calls fulfillment-of-the-other, and the other he just remembers as tasting like Concord grape juice and representing a form of the other. He hasn't lectured or written about them, and so they haven't been tested in the field. Perhaps there aren't thirty-five, but thirty-seven, or more. If there are more, they are presumably of declining usefulness to the bulk of seekers.)

Many, many abstract nouns of value are not included. Where are nobility, patience, generosity, humility, or gentleness? They're kind of tucked in. The brevity of the list is deceiving. It's amazingly economical. Each of the essential aspects contains not just the abstract noun of its name but also other abstract nouns that associate with it, sometimes like a species to a genus. For instance, the noun "discrimination" is a way of experiencing the red body-form, which is usually referred to by the noun "strength." While "strength" is the most commonly noticed feeling connected with the red body-form, at times it appears as the capacity to discriminate. It turns out that strength and discrimination are two ways of looking at the same thing: If strength is the feeling of "I can," then discrimination – parsing the outside world objectively – is the intellectual capability that allows "I can" to arrive. They may not seem to be related nouns at first – strength and discrimination –

but in the deeper reality, they are both included in the constellation of capacity that arrives as the red.

Similarly, the black body-form is usually paired with the abstract noun *power*. But it also contains the concepts "peace" and "stillness." It turns out that inner *power* is still and peaceful, and at times emerges primarily as the feeling of stillness or the feeling of peacefulness. It's still black, and it still knows itself as all three at the same time, as well as anything else within its constellation.

Where there are such sub-nouns related to the essential aspect's capacity, I've tried to include them under the appropriate heading in the catalog that follows. Within the same "constellation" heading I've also included at times other essential aspects that are closely related.

Curiosity/ Joy/Yellow

As one of the five Sufi body-forms, Joy is most often referred to by its color, yellow. The big five body-forms tend to show up vividly in color and saturate the body. They are less likely to show up as a specific foreign body in the torso, although a shape with their color may sometimes appear.

Description of manifest form: Joy generally appears as a pure, canary yellow. It has a bubbly, frothy feeling. Of all aspects, it is probably the lightest. It sometimes appears as a subtle, underlying laugh or persistent giggling. It is often effervescent. It may seem to trigger a strong set of low-amplitude vibrations running through the body. When prominent, joy may saturate the entire internal body as the color yellow.

What it represents: Joy is where everything new starts. It is naïvety, not knowing, curiosity, and beginning. It is also "I want." When a blimp overhead catches your attention, that is joy. It is impulsion, noticing, and not caring. It is free of strategy or concern for consequences. It is simply interested in what is, and exploring what is, exactly as it is. It doesn't mind having attention deficit disorder. Joy doesn't know how to remember or predict. It might be the simplest-feeling form of presence. It both starts everything off, as curiosity, and carries itself along as things are known, as the part of you that knows it doesn't know everything and is open to something beyond what it just learned. It is one of the more vulnerable of the big five body-forms; any thought or effort can stop it.

Its false form: Joy can be manufactured as "going along to get along." Some people are adept at putting up with things through a false cheeriness. But like everyone else they at times resent the control that someone or something else is imposing.

Obstacle in its way: The need to control. The very idea of having needs is an obstacle. When a simple "I want" is replaced by "I expect to get," then the openness of joy is replaced by the mechanics of control, or neurotic need or greed. Joy is often blocked by a resistance to curiosity.

How to encourage the integration of the essential aspect: Spend as long as it takes to appreciate and accept your history of controlling circumstances, your history of experiencing joy, your history of being curious, and your history of turning "I want" into "I need." What is your neediness? Along the way, notice how naïve you can be, how silly, how open, how curious, and how bubbly; try to sustain those feelings and meditate on them as you sustain them. Reward your own playfulness and lightheartedness.

Other nouns within its constellation: Not-knowingness, openness, naïvety, exploration, playfulness, spontaneity, humor

Strength/Red

As one of the five Sufi body-forms, Strength is most often referred to by its color, red.

Description of manifest form: Strength generally appears as a pure, vivid red that can range from dark, blood red to a pale, translucent red. The color often is centered in the lower torso and limbs, or it can suffuse the entire body. The strength aspect has a feeling of a rising, and at times immense, capacity. It is more energetic than most aspects, with medium-amplitude waves that tend to rise from the thighs or belly and gather in the chest, shoulders, and hands. It can appear in jewel form as a ruby. It can be felt to expand beyond the body and can register a sense of boldness, bigness, and aliveness.

What it represents: Strength is the capacity to do things. While joy may represent "I want," strength is clearly "I can." Strength can weaponize us, or it can simply stay latent as an offense or defense ready to be engaged. It is an appreciation of our own capacities, and it is especially present when we feel weak and in need of success. It can manifest as a controlled, appropriate assertion, but without the urgency of instinctual, survival-based aggression. It can also manifest with less energetic force as discrimination, or the ability to see variables and objects clearly and distinctly from each other. In this way, strength includes our ability to analyze, whether intellectually or more subtly.

Its false form: Strength can be manufactured as "pumping up" or "steeling myself." Anger – the defense against being frustrated – is a form of false strength.

Obstacle in its way: The feeling of being weak or stupid. The feeling that others are stronger or smarter, and the desire to give up before trying.

How to encourage the integration of the essential aspect: Spend as long as it takes to appreciate and accept your history of feeling weaker than others, or dumber than others, and being passed over – on the playground, at school, at work, or at home. Along the way, notice how much you have accomplished, how you have risen to the occasion, how you like feeling strong and capable, and how there are things you can do better than other people around you.

Other nouns within its constellation: Discrimination, analysis, capacity, capability, aggression, forcefulness, boldness, courage, expansion, aliveness

Will/White

A s one of the five Sufi body-forms, Will is most often referred to by its color, white.

Description of manifest form: Will may appear in the body as a gleaming white circulating in and around the spine or saturating the body. Its center is the solar plexus, where sometimes it appears as the full moon. (Note: See Universal Will for a related aspect.) It may also appear as pure silver. It feels like an inner support and confidence, or as if grounding isn't under the feet but within the pelvis, like a hill or mountain there. The spine may straighten and be felt as a gleaming rod that stands tall.

What it represents: Will is what propels us to a conclusion. While joy may represent "I want," and strength is "I can," the third of the big five body-forms can be represented by the statement, "I will." It is an inner confidence that needs no outside support. It is related to trust, by requiring surrender of notions that one is helpless alone. Will arrives with a feeling of maturity and steadfastness toward any goal.

Its false form: Willpower is a mechanical set of instructions meant to overcome a fear of laziness. Willpower assumes a stance of mind over matter. It contracts, and includes a feeling of hardness and shutting off of the heart. The iron will.

Obstacle in its way: The belief that I am lazy. The underlying belief is that left to my own devices, I would distract myself with momentary pleasures. I may believe that I am castrated or simply stuck in childishness. It usually includes a feeling that I am incapable of standing on my own two feet and am not a mature being. In absence of innate will, the thought goes, I need to conjure up a better (or more mature) me that will overcome a lazier (or more childish) me. In some cases, this may include a grandiose belief that if not for my laziness I could achieve spectacular results.

How to encourage the integration of the essential aspect: Spend as long as it takes to appreciate and accept your history of feeling lazy, cut off, castrated, spineless, lacking confidence, immature, unable to complete or perfect things, unable to stay on task, or unable to reach your ideal states. Along the way, notice how many accomplishments you have completed, how you have persevered when necessary, how you have no trouble staying on task toward certain goals, and ways in which you feel fully adult.

Other nouns within its constellation: Perseverance, persistence, focus, solidity, groundedness, concentration, maturity, surrender, uprightness, unflappability

Compassion/ Green

As one of the five Sufi body-forms, Compassion is most often referred to by its color, green.

Description of manifest form: An emerald. The green compassion often starts in the chest, as if in the heart, and spreads out through the body or sprays out of the body, as a tender and gentle presence.

What it represents: Compassion allows us to pursue objective inquiry. While joy may represent "I want," and strength is "I can," and will is "I will," the compassion body-form takes us all the way to "I am." This is the "I am" of whatever presence is here now. It includes capacities for sensitivity, openness, empathy, attunement, tenderness, and kindness. When these are all available, the fear of suffering can drop away. Much of our denial of reality as it is involves subtle fears of suffering. While the dimension and presence of will may bring us a kind of support, the compassion sense of support has a feeling of not needing to do anything. Buddhists call this aspect lovingkindness.

Its false form: Sympathy is the most common false sense of compassion. It can be the feeling that since I've experienced that suffering, I know what your suffering is.

Sympathy reinforces the sense of suffering and focuses on the pain rather than what else might be there. Sympathy can also create the belief that I need to do something to fix or correct a suffering, whether yours or mine.

Obstacle in its way: The belief that survival requires me to be hard. Most people believe that "turn the other cheek" is unsafe in some circumstances. Some of the obstacle activities are: Standing your ground, protecting yourself even when actual survival isn't in play, and generally keeping separate and suspicious of others. Anger and emotional suffering.

How to encourage the integration of the essential aspect: Pay attention to the truism that you need to love yourself first. Noticing how your superego attacks you all day long is the first step toward evoking radical self-loving and the compassion body-form. How do you keep your own innate sensitivity and gentleness down? What beliefs do you have about the limits to compassion? How is compassion a substitute for suffering?

Other nouns within its constellation: Lovingkindness, sensitivity, gentleness, self-care, kindness, empathy

Power/Black

As one of the five Sufi body-forms, Power is most often referred to by its color, black.

Description of manifest form: The black of power may feel like a deep, endless void that starts in your forehead or torso and extends down or through and past your body. A profound silence may accompany it, as well as a deep stillness. The blackness is often shiny and can be extremely dense or transparent and empty.

What it represents: Power wipes out the ego's need to know and allows what *is* to instead know itself. While joy may represent "I want," and strength is "I can," and will is "I will," and compassion is "I am," power is "I know." This is a knowingness that lacks emotion or forethought, hindsight or projection. It is profound and clear, engaged without needing anything. This aspect annihilates obstacles and seems to open the mind to vast stores of information. With no conflict to resolve, it can feel like peace, and it can feel perfectly humble.

Its false form: Needing to know and dominate through information is a common substitute for the inner guidance of power. Pride and grandiosity are the false form's attitudes. Hatred and separation are false forms also.

Power and peace are simple unifying forces, while hatred and separation keep a duality prominent.

Obstacles in its way: The belief that I need to be separate. The belief that war is the opposite of peace and is necessary in certain circumstances. The belief that all knowledge is stored in my brain. Identification with powerlessness, and doubt of one's experience.

How to encourage the integration of the essential aspect: What makes you need to be right? What makes you need to toe a line? Power shows up when the dualities right-wrong and good-bad have been deeply explored. Do you need to be kept in line by a code of ethics, for instance, or is there another source of guiding wisdom? What would it take to see through my emotions? This work goes to the heart of listening for the content of the superego voice and questioning its assumptions. If those assumptions were set aside, what else might be seen or known?

Other nouns within its constellation: Peace, humility, stillness, annihilation, depth, mystery, magic

Truth/Gold

T ruth is gold. Anytime the element gold appears in the body during an inquiry, it is essential truth showing itself. It often appears in an alloy, mixed with or next to another emanating aspect. It is expressing the truth of the presence of the other aspect, or the way that aspect participates in truth. So it can appear embodied as a thing itself, or as a proof of the truth of something else.

Description of manifest form: The gold of truth is rich, luminescent, smooth, pure, shiny, and metallic. It is often dense and warm. It may be solid, or it may be fluid. If fluid, it may be still or may flow. It may be alone or accompany other manifestations. It can form itself as a frame or a protector, or as an alloy that adds proof to the experience.

What it represents: This is the truth found in the expression, "The truth shall set you free." It can be the cleansing truth that wipes away distortion, or the purifying truth that removes falsity. It assures the recipient that there is no need to look further, that an accurate and objective description of what is present has shown itself. The truth is so dense and pure that it leaves no room for false forms. It represents our capacity to tell that something is true.

Its false form: As might be expected, the false forms of truth gravitate around lies. These aren't so much overt lies as they are the ego's belief systems that distort reality. Belief systems tend to be seen in the body as structures. They are often made of welded-together bars of steel or other dull metal. The bars may even have a gold luster.

Obstacles in its way: Belief systems that are adopted to fix reality in a manageable place tend to be the main obstacle to truth. Self-deception. Essential truth is accurate, but it is also objective, absent of emotion or need, and able to stand alone. A desire to achieve something often blocks out the possibility of truth for its own sake.

How to encourage the integration of the essential aspect: How willing are you to look into yourself, warts and all? Can you look for the ways you resist, deny, or avoid what's actually going on, in favor of molding a reality that might better please you? The very process of psychological inquiry is the path to the acknowledgement and participation in essential truth. Learning to explore your own hidden deficiencies can release those deficiencies. The truth is that you are perfect, and it takes time and courageous exploration to accept your own participation in God.

Other nouns within its constellation: Spirit, non-judgment, objectivity, accuracy, purity, disidentification

Brilliancy/
Transparent

Description of manifest form: Brilliancy invites comparison to liquid mercury: dense, flowing and shining. It can show up with the explosive light of the sun shining in a mirror. It can be fundamentally white or transparent, but it has a sensation of absolute inclusion, as if everything could be distilled into a single emanation and shine out from the inside. Special effects can include seeing through people around you to their sparkly perfection, as if they are transparent, glimmery bodies that open to multi-faceted, colorful diamonds.

What it represents: Brilliancy is like an essence of essence. It represents the feeling when all aspects – or at least the big five body-forms – are available, present and synthesized into a single awareness. It is as if all the intelligence in the universe is available in a single moment. It can feel like a new brain has shown up that isn't limited in size or function, but that can grok the entire interconnected universe of causes and effects. But it is personal, too, and can only show up when all the big five body-forms have been integrated into the soul. That is, when the student has explored all the big five thoroughly, and felt their presence palpably, then brilliancy may arise, too.

Its false form: Incomplete knowledge of any sort can still feel brilliant. Evangelists and zealots may believe that they are in the presence of a deeper, more complete knowledge. Their need to evangelize betrays the truth, that they are leaving something out.

Obstacles in its way: The belief that I need to know. The belief that I have already articulated the most divine of mysteries. The belief that being farther down a path than others is enough. The belief that I may still have deficiencies – holes to fill – but my mind is clear already. An inability to acknowledge my own history of intelligence.

How to encourage the integration of the essential aspect: Brilliancy tends to naturally arise as the big five body-forms complete their integration into the body. It helps to extinguish the belief that your intelligence can be measured as an IQ.

Other nouns within its constellation: Impeccability, synthesis, intelligence, clarity, precision, completeness, innocence, preciousness

Value/Amber

Description of manifest form: The essential aspect Value is amber. It can be the color amber or the semi-precious stone amber. It may come to you as a sense of deliciousness, felt as a taste. It can seem like a sweet and light dessert.

What it represents: Value is your ground and your inborn perfection. It is the you before the attacks of the superego, the you who has no core needs or deficiencies. Value is the tabula rasa you come into the world with, identical in its perfection with every other baby's. Value is beyond self-esteem; it is who you are, your existence itself. Inherent and primordial worth.

Its false form: When we pump ourselves up, act grandiose, brag, or disparage others, we're trying to overcome a latent sense of deficiency or worthlessness. Anytime we think we can't participate in life coherently without props, we're replacing true value with false value.

Obstacles in its way: The belief that I have essential deficiencies. The superego itself is the primary obstacle to recognizing our inherent value. Emphasis on collecting external things to establish a sense of value.

How to encourage the integration of the essential aspect: Value tends to start making an appearance as the superego's stories recede. The very exploration of worthlessness and deficiency encourages the appearance and recognition of value.

Other nouns within its constellation: Self-love, perfection, existence, self-worth

.

Knowingness/ Blue

Description of manifest form: The essential aspect Knowingness is blue. It is more subtle than most of the divine body-forms and seems almost transparent, like a gas. Its feeling is one of direct contact, immediacy, as if attentive to everything going on right now, all at once. It can be accompanied by a feeling of the top of the cranium disappearing and the head being exposed to the blue sky.

What it represents: Knowingness is pure consciousness. It's the ground of all knowledge as knowable. It's like the felt sense of truth, but it arrives even before truth. It isn't just the potential of knowing something; it's also the knowledge that a concept, a sentence, an experience, a sensation, a meaning are directly contacting you, with no interference. Knowingness gives us the capacity to learn and use all the other essential aspects. When I grok joy or strength, I'm not analyzing them anymore. I'm in Knowingness.

Its false form: Rote knowledge, beliefs, opinions, old ideas, anything stored or taken to have been formed by the conventional mind. These are all convincing, and often practical, false forms of knowingness. Whenever "I know this" is approximately so – I'm 99.9 percent believing it –

then I know I'm in the false form. Knowingness feels more like participation in a consciousness that pervades everything.

Obstacles in its way: Belief that not only is the conventional mind enough, it's all there is in terms of thought, creativity, truth, and success in life. Counter-intuitively, people who trust their minds and have confidence in their mental powers can have a hard time finding their way to Knowingness. Believing that my conventional mind is enough for me to reach my goals – whether material or spiritual – keeps me dissociated from my own Knowingness.

How to encourage the integration of the essential aspect: Knowingness arises when I can question the assumption that the rational human mind, the cranial one that judges the world based upon on agreed-upon logic, is all there is. Is it possible that there's a consciousness deeper than my own rationality? General work on identities and psychodynamic issues also helps: Knowingness shows itself naturally as the essential aspects – the thirty-five divine body-forms – appear. Any experience that helps move the sense of mind out of the cranium and into the heart and body encourages an appreciation of Knowingness.

Other nouns within its constellation: Consciousness, grokking, direct knowing, precision

Personal Love/ Pink

Description of manifest form: I can hardly improve on Ali's description: "It appears in the inner visual sense as a beautiful and luminous pink, either as a shapeless medium or with a shape like a flowing pink stream, a pink cloud, or cotton candy, or a pink rose. It appears in the inner taste sense as a heavenly kind of sweetness, an uplifting taste that makes us realize why we associate love with sweetness. It appears in the inner olfactory sense as the scent of rose or jasmine, delicate and so transporting. It appears in the inner auditory sense as the gentle delicate buzzing of bees, tinkling of bells, or a melodious enchanting sound."[1]

What it represents: Personal Love is the pleasurable experience of being appreciated or appreciating someone or something else. It includes liking and being liked. We need to know ourselves as sweet and to recognize that sweetness as a wonderful state of presence. Love isn't an emotion or an expectation, but a state of essential being.

Its false form: Feeling a need to be wanted is the basic insecurity that drives us toward a false sense of love.

---

[1] A.H. Almaas *Inner Journey Home.* Boston: Shambhala, 2004, p. 136

Obstacles in its way: Love becomes confused with a belief that we need someone to mirror our sweetness in order for it to emerge or take hold. Our own native sweetness needs to be experienced and trusted before we can truly appreciate the similar sweetness in others. Belief that I am unlovable, or that my history is one of being unloved or losing love.

How to encourage the integration of the essential aspect: Pink, fluffy love is relatively easy for many people to discover in themselves. The trick tends to be allowing it to be seen as a mature presence. It may be helpful to study your tendency to relegate pink, fluffy love to childishness, and not see that it is the true adult connecting material.

Other nouns within its constellation: Sweetness, appreciation, self-love, liking, wonderfulness

Passionate Love/ Pomegranate

Description of manifest form: The form of love we call passion emanates as an essential aspect with exotic sweetness, like pomegranate. It often appears as the color of pomegranate and with a sense of taste that is sweet and slightly tart both. It carries many of the sensed qualities of strength, including the feeling of being filled with rich blood and pulsing energy.

What it represents: Passionate love contains the erotic, but it also represents the deeply felt love for God or consciousness. This fiery, consuming, annihilating love empties the heart of distortion. When Christ talks in the Beatitudes of the rich inheritance due the poor in spirit, it is this passion that paves the way.

Its false form: Commonly, people feel a need to bring passion into their lives by finding an object of passion and drawing it close. The false form of divine passion is the kind of passionate love that carries with it a need to merge with another in order to feel complete.

Obstacles in its way: Our Oedipal history tends to be the biggest obstacle. The displacement of erotic love into a desire for return to a faintly remembered early attachment

– often to a mother or father – blocks out the deeper possibility of union with God or consciousness.

How to encourage the integration of the essential aspect: Working on Oedipal issues starts the movement toward essential Passion. After a while, the defenses of the heart will break down, and the possibility of passionate love that goes beyond the attachment to a single person arises. As the heart is seen for what it is, and especially its self-sufficiency, its false contents tend to burn up or disappear.

Other nouns within its constellation: Unity, voluptuous presence, sweet strength, aliveness, consuming love

Universal Love/ Shimmering Transparency

Description of manifest form: Universal Love has a soft and sweet feeling of heartfelt connection with everything, and includes noticing that everything is equal and perfect. This feeling can be accompanied by a sense of generosity and loss of personality. With no separation between things, everything may appear to shimmer with transparency or a delicate light. It is a way of experiencing nondual reality.

What it represents: Universal love is sometimes called cosmic consciousness. It is the term for the lack of separation between things, and the appreciation of the unequivocal beauty of everything and everyone. Unlike personal love, universal love enjoys meeting everything equally, and ascribes no favor.

Its false form: If it feels like you've accomplished something by moving into a sense that everything or everyone is deserving of love, you're still stuck in your personality.

Obstacles in its way: The belief that I am a separate entity. The belief that our original holding environment – parents and home – was deficient is the major obstacle. Hanging onto opinions about our original holding environment tends to create our measure of distrust. The distrust can be toward specific people, types of people, structures in the world, all the way up to our concepts of God and the universe.

How to encourage the integration of the essential aspect: Like Brilliancy, Universal Love tends to appear after many other things have fallen into place. The Jesus way is to focus on forgiveness until it opens to a bigger compassion, and then find a way to trust that you can forgive anything and everything. This is such a radical way of behaving that it may either cause or result from a complete breakdown of the force of the personality.

Other nouns within its constellation: Christ consciousness, cosmic consciousness, harmony, nondual love

Merging Love/ Gold

Description of manifest form: Merging Love feels like melting. Your body can feel like honey, but lighter, with the density of melted butter. A sense of interior and exterior boundlessness is often evoked. It can be a transparent gold fluid that melts what it touches, with an unearthly sweetness.

What it represents: Merging Love represents being at one, without need of a particular other. It is as if nurturing were always available, and the sense of good mother didn't need a physical mother. It is the unity that arises as beliefs in need for an external source for nurturing falls away. With its arrival, fear of vulnerability departs. It provides the capacity for connection, the essence of intimacy, and reflects the loss of separation. It naturally arises in healthy close relationships, whether intimate or familial. It is an underpinning of sharing and of a sense of community.

Its false form: The split-off "good mother" is the shadow form of the pure essence called Merging Love. The desire to fall in love with a nourishing, invulnerable person represents the familiar version of merging love. The neurotic need to be merged with another.

Obstacles in its way: Merging Love appears only when the image of the good mother disappears. As long as the seeker is trying to return to a state of bliss that is remembered through the earliest life with mother, Merging Love is unavailable. Any sense of need for the merging with mother, or the protection of mother, or external nourishment, tends to get in the way of the manifestation of the Merging Love essence. Resistance to merging, connection, and sharing. Belief in need to be separate.

How to encourage the integration of the essential aspect:
Working on what psychologists refer to as "splitting," the common belief system that splits the mother into two memories: all-good mother and all-bad mother. Often the "good mother" idealization is much stickier than the bad mother image. It's hard to let go of the feeling that life is a journey back to that original symbiosis with mother. Seeing through that image as an identity that needs to be clarified may lead first to a feeling of deficient emptiness – depression and meaninglessness – before breaking through to a lower floor, where Merging Love resides. Yearning for and trying to get back to an original mother is a dead end, but exploring the desire for merging can open the door to recognizing it as a quality of your heart.

Other nouns within its constellation: Nourishment, vulnerability, sweetness, connection, sharing, community, melting love

The Point/ Pure Light

Description of manifest form: Essential Identity may appear as a point of light in the body or as a sense of self as a star in a limitless dark sky. As broader dimensions of reality open to us, this aspect allows us to experience them as our identity. This is what is meant by self-realization. It can rest as an infinitesimally bright object, or it can morph into an unbounded abstraction. It can be a point of view, seeing a universe of brilliantly clear objects. Or it can dissolve into the same fullness, or even into a void.

What it represents: Essential Identity is the distilled essence of who we are as individuals, down to a quasi-object that is only a location, or only a sense of presence, or only a drop in a still, boundless, ocean of the absolute. It is the "me" before anything is impressed on "me," and the "me" after every characteristic is removed. It is the unadorned "I am" of Ramana Maharshi. It is the "I am the light" of Jesus. It is the person of Being alone. It represents the truth that spiritual nature is our true identity and being.

Its false form: All of our identities – especially the sticky ones that operate as roles in a stage-crafted life – add up to the immense structure that obscures Essential Identity. The false form may show up materially as a pea in the abdomen, a dry presence that has no value but seems to take up space. True identity is not constructed from past experiences.

Obstacles in its way: Every identity you have is an obstacle to meeting up with the essence of your true identity. They all get in the way: being a father or mother, a trauma victim, a Democrat or Republican, a generous person, a truth-seeker, a lousy athlete, a bad friend, and on and on forever. If "I am" is not a complete sentence for you, anything you end it with (I am a person, I am a cheerleader, I am a good husband, I am a father, I am musical) is an identity.

How to encourage the integration of the essential aspect: Seeing and understanding your own narcissism. The essential identity is realized mostly through the superego work, which is aimed at the removal of identities. Identities imply an attachment to a particular state of being and don't allow the flow to express you and itself as whatever happens in the moment. Identities take a pleasing memory and try to get it to stay in place into the future. Removal of identities is a tedious, time-consuming, fraught process. The biggest pain is that eventually you have to get rid of all the identities you like, too.

Other nouns within its constellation: Meaning, location, singularity, autonomy, uniqueness, timelessness, authenticity

The Pearl/ Milk White

Description of manifest form: The Personal essence typically manifests as a pearl, white sphere, or white ovoid, usually first located in the belly or sternum. It may appear and reappear as a bigger or smaller pearl. It may also expand and stretch through the body as a milky-white essence with a liquid feel. Often it pushes the stomach out, and may be mistaken for a feeling of pregnancy. Like other aspects, it may expand out beyond the limits of the body, in its case as a milky-white cloud, accompanied by a sense of fullness of presence.

What it represents: The personal essence is the unique self that functions in the world as the divine. It expresses the development and individuation of the soul, which is with the body but not of the body. As the distortions of the ego depart, the personal is brought forth and seen. It is the underlying capacity to act without expectation or remorse, and delight in the truth with love. The personal essence is the you of capacities, skills, and understanding that are all part of your development as a human being. It gives us the capacities to be personal and to make contact. It underlies all relating.

Its false form: Your personality is the false form of your person. Your personality, or ego, distorts your view, both in what it sees outside of you and what it believes are your capacities to respond to what is outside of you. The personality is a structure that needs constant propping-up. The pearl always feels adequate through the availability to it of all the other aspects.

Obstacles in its way: Belief in your stories, your thread of life, your memories as harbingers, your need to stick to a point of view, and your reliance on opinion to make your way in the world all block realization of the personal essence. Resistance to being personal, to making genuine contact. Emotional distance or withdrawal.

How to encourage the integration of the essential aspect: The personal essence reveals itself as you continue to undertake an appreciation of the other essential aspects. As they integrate, you start to trust that what you need isn't best filtered through your ego and id but arises naturally through your share of divinity. So studying the essential aspects it the way to the personal essence.[2] It helps to explore our capacities and their seeming limitations in being personal, in contact, or attuned to the uniqueness of others.

Other nouns within its constellation: Personalization, individuation, functioning, soul, effortlessness

---

[2] The point and pearl toggle with each other. As the world unfolds, you participate from a point as a pearl.

Universal Will/
Platinum

Description of manifest form: Universal Will is platinum. Harder, tougher, more solid than the silver of Personal Will, the platinum feels dynamic and supportive. It can feel molten and solid at once. A sense of security tends to accompany the solidity. It may saturate the body, or replace the spine as a platinum bar, or accompany another sensed object. Often it may seem immense, even if trapped in a small space.

What it represents: Universal Will shows us the firmness and purity of an essential support that flows through everything. It reminds us that the universe is its own support and is available to us as a personal support when needed. Universal Will supports your soul in its development, as it supports everything and everyone in and around you. It says to you: Pure beingness does not fail. Your own personal will is a rock on the mountain of universal will.

Its false form: If the universe seems random and as prone to evil as good, then universal will cannot be at play. A malicious God, a Manichean culture, or an "I'm-on-my-own" attitude all represent an aversion to the possibility of universal will. Often the image of a father – forceful or cruel or abusive or weak or in virtually any form – may create a personal drama that obscures the possibility of universal will.

Obstacles in its way: The kind of atheism that rejects the chance that there's a firm underlying essence to everything gets in the way of noticing universal will. Remaining engaged in an internal dialogue with a father may prevent its emergence. For many people, universal will requires working past a subtle feeling that it would be nice for your parents to have continued to support you through life.

How to encourage the integration of the essential aspect: First, work on your relationship with your father or father figures in your early life. Ask yourself about his support for you. Inquire into your beliefs about the solidity and firmness of the universe as a cosmic consciousness. Is it always there, always at the ready? What gets in the way of finding that grounding? Inquire into your attachment to father images; what would life be like if you didn't need them?

Other nouns within its constellation: Support for all, optimization, firmness, solidity, immensity

Sincerity/ Bronze

Description of manifest form: The aspect shows up as bronze with an amber tinge. It is an alloy of truth and strength – gold and red. As a heart essence, it feels fluid and sweet, with a firmness and clarity that suggests its love of integrity.

What it represents: The sincerity aspect underlies a full-blown faithfulness in pursuing the truth, no matter where it might take us. It has no capacity for bending, avoiding, denying, or preventing the truth from being exposed as it is now. It is a particular protection from the distortions that the ego desires and imposes on our truth-seeking. This is the love of the truth. Honesty refers to individual sincere acts. Sincerity is the essence that keeps us honest, and it reflects an overall integrity.

Its false form: Any partial surrendering to the truth, such as bargaining or compromising with it, is a false sincerity. Allowing ourselves to lie to ourselves gives us a structure based on made-up beliefs.

Obstacles in its way: Compromise, dishonesty, denial, and all those sorts of things get in its way. But so do attachment to companionship, hierarchical ethics, and self-disgust, as well as a litany of other ego-based sideshows. More generally, a fear of what you'll see deep inside yourself – worthlessness, pride, greed, any number of self-attacks – can prevent a truth-seeker from taking certain steps toward uncomfortable truths. Spiritual bypass – the rush toward bliss experiences even while the ego is still running the show – is a common method to try to circumvent sincerity.

How to encourage the integration of the essential aspect: There is no way to avoid the work of exposing your own lies. How does your own narcissism get in the way of the truth? When do you let go of your own true sweetness and loving availability?

Other nouns within its constellation: Ruthlessness, integrity, truth, earnestness, authenticity, self-love

Surrender/ Dark Gold

Description of manifest form: Honey, as a dark gold, melting, annihilating substance that works through us from top to bottom.

What it represents: Surrender brings us the capacity to take an attitude without resistance. It isn't piecemeal; it's a complete surrender. It often begins with a yearning for itself and a period of grieving for what is lost as it proceeds. It purges the ego and its demands for defenses and resistance. It evolves into an ego-death that leaves behind honey, buzzing bees, and sweetness. Surrender can lead a person to become an instrument of the divine.

Its false form: Withdrawal as a defense mechanism is the simplest shadow form of true surrender. In other ways, any defense implies a shadow form of surrender. For some people, pride in humility can be its shadow.

Obstacles in its way: Resistance structures in the body, mind, and heart all get in the way of true surrender. These can be defense mechanisms or they can be diversionary tactics.

How to encourage the integration of the essential aspect: Explore the different levels of resistance you put up –

psychological, physical, and soulful. What is it to require defense, and what are your defenses? What would it be like to arrive without defense? To not know beforehand? To be empty-handed? What are the ways you are proud to be who you are? What would life be like without them?

Other nouns within its constellation: Ego-death, not-knowing, defenselessness, openness, self-sufficiency

Melting/ Soft Yellow

Description of manifest form: Butter in the act of melting: changing shape and losing solidity while retaining a liquid substantiality. Constant motion of solid to liquid. It is a complete melting of the entire being, not isolated to the heart or a place in the body, and it is continual, non-stop, without conditionality.

What it represents: This is beyond the act of surrender into something. This is constant surrender as a way of life, as a defenseless posture that constantly melts away the past, both long ago and momentary, and enters fluidly, without structure.

Its false form: Melting is a middle state; it's neither solid nor liquid. It's always in between. The false forms of this aspect include a feeling of need to retain solidity or of having been left a helpless pool. It can emerge as victimized resignation.

Obstacles in its way: Holding on to the belief in a need for resistance. Any rigidity of belief or identity will stop the action of melting. Superego demands for structured identities and beliefs will block you from continual melting. Men may feel that the yielding sense of melting threatens masculinity. Women may feel in turn that it is too accommodating. So protection of false strength is a primary obstacle. In fact, this kind of melting surrender requires enormous courage and trust.

How to encourage the integration of the essential aspect: What are your beliefs as you fall asleep? They're not there. Can you be like that in broad daylight? You can have beliefs, but can you let them come and go as they wish, rather than trying to pin them down? The Byron Katie method of inspecting your beliefs and discovering that they don't need to be fixed is a practice that can lead to melting. But beware: This constant relaxation of identity and beliefs is almost intolerable to the superego. It will fight hard to maintain its beloved structures. Control becomes the central issue to consider: How do I let go of control and slide into the flow of the emerging moment? The Melting aspect can emerge as a practical bridge between experiences of transcendent formlessness and activities of daily life.

Other nouns within its constellation: Surrender, dis-identification, relaxation, doubt

Vulnerability/ Water/Uncolored

Description of manifest form: Water that moves passively and gently, without much force, almost without notice. It has no taste, no scent, nothing that leans it one way or another.

What it represents: This aspect allows you to be and let yourself be, passively, unnoticed and unremarkable. What are you as purely human, before an impression has made a mark? Being human is not much more than being impressionable. Being impressionable is a kind of passive vulnerability that accompanies us at all times. Integration of this aspect leaves you willing to be just a regular Joe and to stop seeking exceptional experiences, or better ones than the ones you've already experienced. You don't need drama, and you don't need excitement. By metaphor, if the universe is in constant flux, it may flow through you without resistance. You're open to change.

Its false form: False humility or accommodation may arise as ego techniques to feign vulnerability when a threat is coming.

Obstacles in its way: Belief in emotional drama as a sustaining presence gets in the way of approaching the world with an objective, untilted outlook. Self-protection

implies a need for something better than what is
happening now, and a rejection of the present as
undesirable. What we're avoiding is the chance that
something we have labeled as "bad" will enter us and leave
an impression or stale taste.

How to encourage the integration of the essential aspect:
Inquire into your need to protect yourself by amping your
life up. How do you avoid being ordinary? What would you
feel like if it was OK to be boring? Is it enough to just be
human? If the impressions were safe, could you allow
yourself to be constantly impressionable?

Other nouns within its constellation: Ordinariness,
allowance, malleability, humanness

Acceptance/ Aquamarine

Description of manifest form: It has a feeling of contentment without needing any specific object of contentment. It is light and delicate, and if it arises as a crystal, it's as if the edges are melting while the crystal shimmers. Even just the aquamarine color can bring a smile.

What it represents: Acceptance is the process of mind and heart that doesn't try to correct the world as it is unfolding. It might still contain preferences for action, but they don't interfere with an accurate inclusion of everything that is actually happening. This kind of acceptance is notable for being total and absolute; it leaves no room for resistance. Rejection is not necessary when it's all right to accept life as it truly is. Acceptance feels like there's room around everything, including things that you might love and things you might ignore. You might notice equanimity; it doesn't distinguish between favorable and unfavorable.

Its false form: When acceptance is begrudging, it assumes that rejection is also possible and real. When acceptance is partial or only offered to favorites, then you're still working within your ego system.

Obstacles in its way: Protecting the ego through denial, resentment, and other forms of rejection is the primary obstacle to the discovery of true acceptance. The belief that the ego structures keep you safe prevent real acceptance. The ego bases its conceptual distinctions on threats and resistance to threats. Acceptance starts from neutrality and contentment, not threat.

How to encourage the integration of the essential aspect: Most of the work is simply drilling into the ego's belief that the universe needs to be divided into things to accept and things to reject. Seeing through the false assumptions that create rejection tends to help them fall away. Working through rejection, especially rejection in relationships.

Other nouns within its constellation: Space, roominess, comfort, contentment, equanimity, lightness, openness

Spirituality/ Saffron

Description of manifest form: In color, scent, and taste, the saffron essence evokes the spice. It's a rich red-yellow. It arises with a feeling of contentment. A sense of relaxation can accompany it as it settles into a chosen way of being.

What it represents: The saffron essence represents the love of the spiritual and the presence of the spiritual at the same time. It is the contentment that shows up when one enters the kingdom of heaven. It incorporates the movement into the spiritual as a preferred way of life, and a place to be relaxed.

Its false form: Any fixed notion of what nirvana or enlightenment is supposed to be like is a false form of the saffron essence. Heaven as a place in the sky to be met only after death is a false form.

Obstacles in its way: Whenever the spiritual path becomes goal-oriented toward a paradise that is better than what is here today, the possibility of heaven already being here right now departs. Fixed notions of heaven, particularly as a paradise of pleasing objects, prevent the inner heaven from being appreciated. Wanting heaven to make everything better gets in the way, too.

How to encourage the integration of the essential aspect: Explore your notions of heaven and paradise. Are you OK with heaven being ordinary and here around you now? Is spirituality for its own sake, and not to get to a destination that's better, OK with you?

Other nouns within its constellation: Contentment, heaven, path, enlightenment, paradise

Ridhwan/ Contentment/ Persimmon

Description of manifest form: A juicy persimmon conjures this aspect, but as if a nectar more than the fruit itself. It might be a smooth and luminous syrup, pink and gold and yellow at once.

What it represents: This aspect is quite subtle. It is a form of contentment that is accompanied by a feeling of fulfillment. The contentment is in a way for the sake of contentment itself and not reflecting any particular station or series of events. "Ridhwan" is Arabic for this merging of contentment that includes a sweet feeling inside and a feeling of contentment for everything outside at the same time. Heaven is inside *and* outside in this aspect. This isn't the acceptance of paradise's existence; it's the rich, contented feeling of fulfillment when paradise is evoked. It is both fulfilled and fulfilling. It can also represent the archangel guardian of paradise.

Its false form: Any contentment that reflects a potential or actual discontent is the mind's shadowy version of this subtle aspect. Feeling content *for something* is not the same as feeling content for the divinity within and without.

Obstacles in its way: The notion that contentment is variable and depends on outside circumstances gets in the way of this. We believe in our own discontents. We believe that others are just as discontented. We don't see that presence itself opens up a fulfillment that has no object, no purpose, and no barrier.

How to encourage the integration of the essential aspect: Explore your notions of what it takes to feel contentment and fulfillment. And how your full heart wants that for others, too. Open and ripen that heart. What if contentment and fulfillment were always readily available, for you and for others? How would that change your notions of compassion and self-love? What rules for contentment did you learn as a child?

Other nouns within its constellation: Equanimity, fulfillment, divinity, richness

Impersonality/ Uncolored

Description of manifest form: Vast, dark, silent emptiness. Ali calls it the Brahman after the Hindu word for absolute reality.

What it represents: A witness that is objective, part of any experience, impersonal, and always available to me. It doesn't carry any characteristics or biases, but helps with the awareness of what is actually going on around us. It is a vast, eerie, dark space in which everything happens. In it, you can witness the totality of your personal life without involvement, engagement, or reaction.

Its false form: Our internal observer is an extension of the ego, either supporting the ego (which also speaks for the id) or the superego. It is culturally biased, tends to be afraid, and limits our view to variables that support its need for safety and its deeply felt fear of death.

Obstacles in its way: Self-protection, pride, collected knowledge, and all the grasping of the superego create identities that obscure our natural witness. Attachment to the particulars of your personal life.

How to encourage the integration of the essential aspect:
As various dis-identifications proceed, over time space
opens for a different and silent witness who doesn't have a
dog in the fight.

Other nouns within its constellation: Space, vastness,
non-engagement, non-enmeshment

Nourishment/ Translucent White

Description of manifest form: Slightly sweet milk may seem to arise in the mouth or anywhere in the body. It may be the consistency of mother's milk, or a thicker nectar, often a translucent white, sometimes cast with a little yellow or pink. An udder may present itself. A feeling of gentleness accompanies the nourishment aspect.

What it represents: Soul food! Just as our bodies need the right amount of the right kind of food, so do our souls. As you proceed down a path of truth-seeking or spiritual awakening, how do you see the material of your life? What's the balance between your attention to your new possibilities and your fallback on old habits? How much new do you let in? How often? True new experiences and their understanding are the soul's nourishment. Truth is the primary nutrient. This aspect expresses the ready availability of what we need to learn and grow into a mature human being.

Its false form: Any imbalanced sense of spiritual development rests in a belief that you are an object trying to better itself. The idea that reading some spiritual books, or even a lot of books, will bring on enlightenment is a typical false nourishment. Dividing the world into

Neal Allen

instructional or nourishing moments and boring or starved moments.

Obstacles in its way: Believing that nourishment comes primarily from outside us. Often, early issues with the mother as provider and nurturer block access. At first, the main obstacle is the superego's claim that self-inquiry is selfish and prideful. Or that being on a spiritual path is weird. How do you feed something you're fighting against?

How to encourage the integration of the essential aspect: Pay attention to your spiritual appetites. Are you greedily heading down a route that feeds your ego more than your essential self? Why do you back away from the hard parts like a child avoiding the less sweet, salty or fatty vegetables? What else would be good to add to or remove from your diet?

Other nouns within its constellation: Growth, development, balance, education, metabolization

Space/
Clear or Dark

Description of manifest form: Beginning as a tingling at the top of the head, Space develops into the sensation of an opening, as if the cranium cleaves. The hole in the top of the head may become a column that moves up toward the sky. The interior is empty. The space may become clear, empty, luminous and/or dark.

What it represents: Space signals change, emptying past beliefs and allowing the self-image to disappear. Inner spaciousness arises as ego structures move out of the way. Space opens up the possibility of boundlessness and of looking at things fresh, without a rigid viewpoint. This aspect of the divine corresponds to the headless Buddha.

Its false form: Before finding space in the head, many people first encounter a deficient emptiness in the genital region. This sense of castration – male or female – is felt as a troubling inability to find that part of the body, as if it never existed.

Obstacles in its way: The basic identities of being a body – having a body image – and being a collection of impressions and images – being an object in the world that needs support – block us from our share of the divine.

Believing that our body and our sense of self are under attack stops us from starting over, from a delicious, empty space.

How to encourage the integration of the essential aspect: Confront body-image issues, up to and including the fear of disappearing sexuality. Deeper still is the sense of a permanent deficient emptiness – the reality of seeing through our ego identities – which requires extensive exploration of the superego's beliefs and demands.

Other nouns within its constellation: Void, inner space, boundlessness, emptiness

Gratitude/ Gold-Brown

Description of manifest form: Gratitude takes some of its presence from the gold of Merging Love, and also from Satisfaction, which has the brown-gold color of dates. Gratitude has a juicy fullness to it.

What it represents: Gratitude is the soul's recognition that things are working, and that the soul is learning and pushing through its lessons. Understanding what is working leads to gratitude. It doesn't matter whether on the surface the event was a happy or an unhappy circumstance. All Gratitude cares about is that you understood and worked your way to the next moment. It brings closure to the past, and allows the next moment to enter freshly, without encumbrance.

Its false form: Most of us believe that gratitude is something that is deserved. Your friend deserves your gratitude when she does you a favor. So only events that support your happy structures are eligible. In the false form, an uncomfortable event is undesirable and deserving of hostility, not gratitude.

Obstacles in its way: Taking things for granted gets in the way of gratitude, as do comparison, jealousy and envy.

Resisting separation and your own autonomy can get in the way of gratitude.

How to encourage the integration of the essential aspect:
Notice how you distinguish between what deserves gratitude and what deserves contempt or denial or ignoring. What if you could be grateful for the harshest events, so long as you learned what they were fully? Can you be grateful for what you learned from an abusive parent, a near-death experience, a crippling disease?

Other nouns within its constellation: Fulfillment, satisfaction, contentment, thankfulness, acceptance

Satisfaction/ Brown-Gold

Description of manifest form: Satisfaction has the burnished brown color, sweet taste, and gentle aroma of dates, while the texture has been smoothed into a pudding. It has a close relationship with a feeling of contentment. It is often felt in or near the heart. It is a component of the Gratitude aspect, which mixes it with the gold of Merging Love.

What it represents: Just what it sounds like. This is the ability to let things alone as they are, what the Buddhists describe as a state of equanimity. It often appears as self-satisfaction, which is the simple noticing that you're OK and fine as is, that right now your needs are fulfilled, and you are bereft of drama.

Its false form: The child stomping his feet and crying out, "I'm *fine!*" The feeling of having just gotten something you wanted, before the let-down period begins.

Obstacles in its way: As is true with the Gratitude aspect, the belief that we need to merge with our parents stops us from being OK while alone. (Gratitude merges Satisfaction with Merging Love.) Other beliefs of deficiency and need for external support will raise dissatisfaction with how things are now.

How to encourage the integration of the essential aspect:
Working through parental issues and more generally
through feelings and identities of insecurity (in other
words, all the ego work!) results in the possibility of
recognizing your own satisfaction with what is, as it is.

Other nouns within its constellation: Contentment,
equanimity, gratitude

Transparency/ Clear

Description of manifest form: A feeling, particularly in the head, of cleared-out space, bright-eyed and bushy-tailed, shining with luminous clarity. Sometimes there is the appearance of a thin glass, barely translucent, heading toward pure transparency. Objects appear as if bathed in clear light, and images inside and out are pointed and well-defined.

What it represents: Awakening to objectivity. Precision in thought and understanding. The choice to inquire accurately rather than letting things go, avoiding or denying through vagueness. The use of the head center as a crystalline tool to serve the truth residing in the heart center. It is often the precursor to the appreciation of the aspect of Value.

Its false form: "A sharp tongue." Rigid beliefs that substitute for truthful inquiry may appear to be pointed and sharp, but only in their own defensiveness. When disengagement from the Clear essence is noticed, the head may be surrounded by a thick, dull, and dark sheath.

Obstacles in its way: The idea that truth is a mental function that rests on an elaborate structure of pattern recognition separated from the heart or soul. Narcissism and grandiosity, or their opposites such as belief in having a deficient IQ. Conformity, especially fears that inquiry will disrupt the natural order.

How to encourage the integration of the essential aspect: Investigating the thickness and dullness around the head. This is one of those aspects that are released down the line, after a lot of ego work. Feelings of mental inferiority can be traced to childhood interactions. Learning to recognize how object relations interfere with reality opens the door to clarity, precision, and objectivity.

Other nouns within its constellation: Precision, objectivity, awakening, clear light

Fulfillment/ Apricot

Description of manifest form: The color and nectar of an apricot, in all its juiciness, sweetness, and redolence. The nectar may emerge in your body or fall on you in a light rain. Delight and fullness of heart often accompany the sense of the nectar. This aspect often evokes a feeling of bliss, the kind that sweeps the body with waves of pleasure and settles in the heart.

What it represents: This is the recognition that the path or process toward self-realization is on course and working. You both feel that it's working and feel the dynamism of the work itself. You feel optimized suddenly. You may notice the optimizing principle is at work and paradise is attainable. (There was a time I remember when it seemed as if the heaven without had emerged within. That moment, and others like it when I recognized the work of the path, came with a soft, thrilling contentment.) It is a heart quality.

Its false form: Feeling fulfilled by external things, rather than the ripening of the heart. This simple sense of appreciation for the fulfillment of what once was a dream seems childish to the ego. In its desire to control, the ego equates fulfillment with a brutal, Oedipal desire to out-mature your central father figure. Maturation into a being who can control the world at will is the shadow's model. Not realizing that fulfillment is not an emotion but an essential presence with a quality of sweetness and fullness of love.

Obstacles in its way: Feeling the need to merge with mother and not individuate can get in the way of essential fulfillment. Because fulfillment is associated with the personal essence (the pearl), it raises questions of maturity. If we're faking life with notions such as "work is what identifies me and brings me fulfillment," then we're not going to find a deeper source for fulfillment.

How to encourage the integration of the essential aspect: This aspect like some others tends to arise on its own, at an appropriate place, without a lot of prodding. It often arises at the point of rest in a stage of a spiritual path. You've completed a set of learnings, or you're seeing a new path that you will be entering soon. To be ready for it to appear, though, you might explore your preconceptions about fulfillment and how they resonate with ego demands for meaning, completion, crossing barriers, and worthiness. Another question to ask: Do you deserve to be rewarded for your work? Finally, you probably will need to resolve your natural tension between wanting to be merged with a mother figure and wanting to be autonomous and individuated. Can you find both at once, or can you live without either as a demand?

Other nouns within its constellation: Ecstasy, fruition, bliss, maturity, completion

Forgiveness/ Turquoise

Description of manifest form: Its color is a light and soft turquoise. Its feeling is nearly weightless, clean, and soft. It is often felt in the heart center, replacing the leaden weight of its protective opposite, emotional pain. It can feel like your heart is open to the skies and filled with turquoise light. It often has a holy feel. There's a sense of knowingness, and a feeling of freshness.

What it represents: Forgiveness is the capacity to accept past wrongs, difficulties, and hurts. It helps bring the past into the present of Being. If not for forgiveness, past hurts might stay attached and disrupt our ability to be in the now. This isn't being good, a moral form of forgiveness. This is the lighthearted feeling that you are free of all grudges. This kind of forgiveness is absolute; once it settles in, revenge stops being of interest. Past infractions are forgotten before they're stored, so the present can stay pure.

Its false form: Ethically based forgiveness is selective and with a hardened layer of moral superiority masks a continuing desire for revenge.

Obstacles in its way: Guilt and self-blame. Vengeance, the eye-for-an-eye desire to inflict the same suffering on someone you blame for your suffering, is the primary obstacle. Vengeance is the opposite of forgiveness. A natural tendency to hide our hatreds, even from ourselves, prevents us from seeking the true form of forgiveness.

How to encourage the integration of the essential aspect: Work through your sense of guilt and blame, including self-blame. It is helpful to bring our desire for revenge to the surface. Often cultural norms require us to stuff these feelings. We don't know how much hatred we contain. Exploring your history of dealing with vengeance, grudges, hatred, and enemies can open up its flimsiness. Practice letting go of a grudge and see whether you've opened yourself to harm.

Other nouns within its constellation: Openness, compassion, knowingness, acceptance, simplicity of the now

Death Space/
Black

Description of manifest form: Deep, dark, endless blackness. Hollow and often foreboding, with a sense of aloneness and eeriness.

What it represents: Without dying, we can experience death from the perspective of a soul seeing itself without body (or, by inference, ego). One form of ego-death is the realization of a life without a body. The defenses of the ego are supported by a fear of bodily death. The ego can crumble with an acceptance of the mortality of the body as natural and not deserving of fear. This space tends to arise at the time of physical death, though it can be experienced earlier as a death for the ego.

Its false form: Denial of feeling, pleasure, or pain separates us from feeling our bodies. We can numb our awareness of our body to the point that we deprive it, or we can do the opposite and demand that the pleasures of the body be supported willy-nilly.

Obstacles in its way: Denial of death and our mortality. As long as the ego is thriving, experiencing death as an essential aspect won't happen. Working through the issues of the ego allow the possibility to visit the death space.

Once appreciated, the tendency to identify with the body may disappear.

How to encourage the integration of the essential aspect: You might want to spend a lot of time in the presence of your concepts of death, your fears of death, and your possible belief that the only absolute is death. Who might be telling your soul these tales? As fear of death relaxes, the ability to experience it increases.

Other nouns within its constellation: Weightlessness, the void, non-attachment, non-identification, absolute loss

Impeccability/ Silver

Description of manifest form: Impeccability can feel like mercury, as a concentrated drop or sphere in the belly center, or related to will as a substance flowing into and through the spine. It is like shiny stainless steel, hard or fluid. It is closely related, also, to the feeling of presence itself, which can be energetic, since it often manifests when disciplining oneself to sustain presence while engaged in everyday pursuits.

What it represents: Impeccability is the willingness to do the continuous work to form an attachment to presence and the deeper realities, rather than letting the attachments to ego structures continue. It represents the discipline that takes on a feeling of constant self-inquiry even while life is continually interrupted. Grace is a wonderful thing, but it can remain invisible if the seeker doesn't have an attitude of preference for presence over distraction.

Its false form: Gritting your teeth or clenching your fists and taking it. Willpower and self-browbeating in the service of the path can fool people into believing that they're good soldiers on the path. An attitude of "fake it until you make it" can obscure a deeper source of discipline. The path requires constant vigilance, especially in the early years when that vigilance and return to self-inquiry is foreign and disturbing to the ego structures.

Obstacles in its way: The biggest obstacle is everyday life. You're probably used to functioning unconsciously, as if you're being guided by memories and threats, and that's enough to get you through whatever's next. Or you like distracting yourself with novels or gossip or video games. Paradoxically, novels and gossip and video games can be great platforms for proper self-remembering, in which you're aware of the presence that accompanies even these everyday behaviors. Laziness and cynicism obscure it.

How to encourage the integration of the essential aspect: Ask yourself what distracts you from your inquiry practice. What distracts you from noticing presence even in the most mundane circumstances? How much do you really believe that grace can give you the ability to find something of rich, deep interest even in the everyday and the moments of suffering? Concentration meditations are supportive, as well as body-sensing routines. They self-amplify, and the discipline required becomes known as the aspect of impeccability, and becomes more available as a backdrop support.

Other nouns within its constellation: Attention, discipline, path

Anointment/ Olive Oil

Description of manifest form: This aspect has all the physical properties of olive oil. It is viscous and translucent, seems to hold its own internal light, ranges in color from greenish to amber to clear, all at once, and provides warmth. It is fluid and pure.

What it represents: The pure and sacred entry into the soul. The oil anoints in honor of being touched by the purity of entering life through the soul instead of the contaminated ego. Being anointed is being chosen, but this isn't a proactive blessing; it's more a reward for letting go, and trusting in the divine. Christ was anointed in preparation for the Transfiguration. Olive oil throughout history has been respected for its ability to keep a flame lit. The oil itself is produced by crushing a bitter olive until its bitterness and hardness are replaced by sweetness and a fluid catalyst for nourishment. The essential aspect recognizes that we have joined the path of the soul that is holy, cleansing, and incorruptible.

Its false form: Any opaque coating to the defensive ego. Armor. Rewarding yourself as if the path is complete. Spiritual materialism.

Obstacles in its way: Declaring victory over the ego before enough of the ego identities have been sidelined prevents this aspect from springing forth. Fearing loss or the guilt of leaving people behind may block you from feeling the sacred purity of entering the realm of the incorruptible soul.

How to encourage the integration of the essential aspect: Keep on working on purification of the soul, however that manifests. It can be disidentification, or letting go of attachments, or integrating other essential aspects. All of those teachings and processes scrape away impurities from the soul. Once the soul is pure, olive oil can be poured. Often this essential aspect is noticed as a kind of marker, passing from the corruptible life to the purity and sanctity of the soul life.

Other nouns within its constellation: Purification, incorruptibility, cleansing, blessing

Existence/ Coal Black

Description of manifest form: A dense and immense mountain, often found in the lower abdomen but also available sometimes outside the body. Its sense of existence cannot be denied.

What it represents: The true existence of being or spirit. That being has its own felt and real existence independent of mind and belief systems.

Its false form: Ego existence. The familiar sense of self that is dependent on history, is inferred through stories and beliefs, and is not directly known.

Obstacles in its way: The belief in our ordinary view of existence and that of the world. This is one of the more abstract, empty essential aspects that require a substantial amount of space having already opened up. Space opens up when identities are seen through.

How to encourage the integration of the essential aspect: Confront the false existence of the ego self.

Other nouns within its constellation: Support, immensity, respect

A Final Note

Until 2010 I was uneasy with the term "soul." What's a soul? Can you measure it? Can you see it? Can you define it? Add a tone of belligerence, and those questions were mine. And then one day, I had an experience like the one that Annie describes in the foreword. I was in a private session with a teacher in the Ridhwan School founded by Hameed Ali. I came across a white egg in my belly, with no shell but white through and through, that slowly expanded until it filled my torso and then softly broke through my skin, into the room, and out. I was a white blob floating in space for a minute or two.

When I eventually came to, my teacher Blanchefleur said in a blasé voice, "You know what that was, don't you, Neal?"

"No."

"That was your pearl. You'll be studying it at your next Diamond Heart retreat."

Something in me shifted. I didn't have to study it. I had it, inside me. It had been there all along. From that day since, I haven't been afraid of the word "soul." I hope you find your pearl.

Shapes of Truth

Acknowledgments

This project began with an email to Hameed Ali expressing dismay that the world hadn't noticed his discovery of a missing link to the Platonic forms. He agreed that his find deserved a book, but said he had other subjects to write about. He offered to help me, and so he has, enormously, especially in the early stages. As the book germinated and took shape in multiple drafts, poor Plato gradually was relegated to a single chapter. Despite that, the book continues to owe its heart to Hameed, and I hope he will forgive me the change in course.

Thank you to Byron Brown for designating me a Ridhwan Scholar so I could have access to the archives of Hameed's talks, which were of invaluable assistance as I researched the thirty-five body-forms.

Along with Hameed, I've had several teachers who turned my interest toward this book's spiritual themes. In the book I mention Florentin and Blanchefleur from the Ridhwan School. Thank you to my Diamond Heart guides, teachers and fellow students. Special nod to the brilliant

Steven Forrest, whose ideas and heart can push me farther than anyone on earth.

The late Robert Birnbaum will always be my primary teacher. I hope I do justice to the part of him that lives on in me.

My clients are a constant thrill ride through these body-form territories. Siobhán McCann and Sana Milošević were my pioneers, guiding me through some incredible wanderings around the universe.

My writing and editing friends came through every time I asked. Special thanks to Carol Guensburg for lucid comments on an early draft. My dear friend Meg Lundstrom provided her brilliant notes for at least three drafts. Grammatically superior, my brother Kent saved me from dozens of embarrassments.

My incredible agent, Sarah Chalfant of the Wylie Agency, landed this book twice!

Finally, there's Annie at my side with her pen and heart, both of which are more refined than any other I know. If everybody had an Annie, the world would be a much better and more loving place, and lots funnier.

Index
Of Body-Forms

Shapes of Truth

Made in the USA
Las Vegas, NV
29 June 2021